ARTS FESTIVALS IN THE UK

This report was commissioned
and funded by the former Office
of Arts and Libraries now part of
The Department of National Heritage

Informing policy by establishing facts

The Policy Studies Institute (PSI) is Britain's leading independent research organisation undertaking studies of economic, industrial and social policy, and the workings of political institutions.

PSI is a registered charity, run on a non-profit basis, and is not associated with any political party, pressure group or commercial interest.

PSI attaches great importance to covering a wide range of subject areas with its multi-disciplinary approach. The Institute's 40+ researchers are organised in teams which currently cover the following programmes:

Family Finances and Social Security
Health Studies and Social Care
Innovation and New Technology
Quality of Life and the Environment
Social Justice and Social Order
Employment Studies
Arts and the Cultural Industries
Information Policy
Education

This publication arises from the Arts programme and is one of over 30 publications made available by the Institute each year.

Information about the work of PSI, and a catalogue of available books can be obtained from:

Marketing Department, PSI
100 Park Village East, London NW1 3SR

Arts Festivals in the UK

Heather Rolfe

POLICY STUDIES INSTITUTE
100 PARK VILLAGE EAST, LONDON NW1 3SR

The publishing imprint of the independent
POLICY STUDIES INSTITUTE
100 Park Village East, London NW1 3SR
Telephone: 071-387 2171; Fax: 071-388 0914

© Policy Studies Institute 1992

ISBN 0 85374 544 7

Report No. 744

A CIP catalogue record of this book is available from the British Library.

1 2 3 4 5 6 7 8 9

How to obtain PSI publications
All book shop and individual orders should be sent to PSI's distributors:

BEBC Distribution Ltd
P O Box 1496, Poole, Dorset, BH12 3YD

Books will normally be despatched in 24 hours. Cheques should be made payable to BEBC Distribution Ltd.

Credit card and telephone/fax orders may be placed on the following freephone numbers:

FREEPHONE: 0800 262260 FREEFAX: 0800 262266

Booktrade Representation (UK & Eire)
Book Representation Ltd
P O Box 17, Canvey Island, Essex SS8 8HZ

PSI Subscriptions
PSI Publications are available on subscription.
Further information from PSI's subscription agent:

Carfax Publishing Company Ltd
P O Box 25, Abingdon OX10 3UE

Laserset by Policy Studies Institute
Printed in Great Britain by Billing & Sons Ltd, Worcester

Contents

Introduction 1
  Background: the diversity of arts festivals 1
  Methods of the study 2
    The postal survey 2
    Regional distribution 3
    Folk festivals 3
    Interviews with festival organisers 4
    The importance of arts festivals 5
  The report 6

1 Arts Festivals in the UK: Background and Objectives 7
  Introduction: the origins and development of arts festivals 7
    The variety of arts festivals 9
  Festival objectives 12
  Key points 14

2 The Festival Programme and Festival Artists 16
  Introduction: the festival programme 16
  Festival art forms 18
    Orchestral, choral and chamber/soloist performances 18
    Jazz performances and jazz festivals 19
    Literature events and literature festivals 19
    Film screenings and film festivals 20
    Drama, mime, cabaret and comedy 20
    Folk festivals and folk performances 21
    Fringe festivals 22
  Children's events 22
  Educational content 22
  Decisions on the artistic programme 26
  Use of themes 28
  Commissioning and innovation 29

Festival artists 31
   Professionals 31
   Amateurs 32
   Collaboration between professional and amateur performers 33
Key points 34

3 The Festival Audience 37
Ticket sales and attendances at free events 37
The festival audience 39
Media coverage 44
   Radio and television coverage 45
Key points 46

4 Festival Staffing 48
Introduction 48
Staff and volunteers 50
Limitations on the use of volunteers 52
Training and management needs of arts festivals 54
Key points 56

5 Funding 57
Introduction 57
Support from arts funding bodies 59
Local authority support for arts festivals 61
   Experiences of local authority support 61
Business sponsorship of arts festivals 63
   Experiences of business sponsorship 64
Other sources of income 67
Festival expenditure 68
   Changes in sources of income 69
Limitations on funding and spending priorities 69
Key points 70

6 The Future of Arts Festivals 73
Festivals' evaluation methods 73
Priorities for development 74
Venues 75
International developments 77
Festivals' plans for change 79

The optimism of festival organisers 79
Conclusions 82
Key points 83

References 85

Appendix 1   Postal questionnaires to arts festivals and folk festivals

Appendix 2   Estimation of totals

Tables

1   Festivals responding to the survey 3
2   Number of festivals per head of population, by country and English region 4
3   Year of origin of arts festivals 8
4   Duration of festivals, by festival type 10
5   Festivals by month held 11
6   Festivals' coverage of art forms 16
7   Art forms and performances/ events by festival type 17
8   Year of origin of jazz festivals 19
9   Number of performances and events at literature and film festivals 20
10   Funding of festivals with an educational component 23
11   Festivals adopting an annual theme 28
12   Funding of festivals commissioning new work 30
13   Festival artists by festival type 31
14   Festivals with ticket sales over 100,000 (1991) 37
15   Distribution of festival ticket sales 37
16   Tickets sold by type of festival 38
17   Festivals with more than 100,000 attendances at free events 38
18   Staffing of arts festivals 48
19   Number of paid staff employed by arts festivals 49
20   Main sources of income by festival type 57
21   Range in total income of arts festivals 58
22   Festivals with an accumulated deficit, by type of festival 58

Acknowledgements

The importance of arts festivals to the cultural life of the UK has been recognised in a number of PSI reports on the arts. Earlier studies on arts centres, amateur arts, and the economic importance of the arts (Hutchison and Forester, 1987; Hutchison and Feist, 1991; Myerscough et al., 1988) have referred to the growth, diversity and significance of festivals. This report is therefore the result of a long-standing interest in arts festivals at PSI.

PSI is greatly indebted to the administrators, organisers and directors of the many festivals who responded to the survey, and particularly of the 16 selected for interview. They are Joseph Allard, Sophie Black, Alan Brack, Sheila Colvin, Frances and Dick Dixon, Nick Dodds, William Dodds, Trish Emblem, Paul Gudgin, Steve Heap, Evan Jones, Kath March, Paul Preager, Dusty Rhodes, Addai Sebo, Jim Wallace and Sheila Whittaker. Their experiences and views are an invaluable addition to the study. Thanks are also due to the British Arts Festivals Association and particularly to its co-ordinator, Gwyn Rhydderch, for advice and assistance with the study.

A number of people at PSI assisted at various stages of the research. Robert Hutchison was responsible for initiating and directing the research, Michael White gave advice and guidance on the analysis of survey data, and Helen Kinnings and Paul Stanaway helped process the survey data. PSI is also grateful to Valerie Tayler, student at North London Polytechnic on placement at PSI, for assistance with the survey and analysis of the survey response rate. Responsibility for the report and its conclusions is, however, that of the author alone.

Introduction

Background: the diversity of arts festivals

Since 1945 arts festivals have become a prominent feature of cultural life in the United Kingdom. Over 500 arts festivals take place each year and there are many hundreds more one-day local and community festivals and carnivals. This report is concerned only with festivals that last for more than a day and that contain some professional input, either artistic or organisational. Apart from their proliferation, the most obvious feature of arts festivals is their diversity in size, content and professional input. Survey data shows that 62% of arts festivals are professionally organised, but 38% are run by unpaid staff. Some festivals, such as the Edinburgh International Festival and the Edinbugh Festival Fringe, run for a number of weeks, but a substantial proportion (26%) of festivals take place over a weekend, and the majority of these are folk festivals. Some festivals, particularly those which are held in large cities, attract audiences of many thousands; for example, the Notting Hill Carnival attracts an estimated 1.5 million participants, while others draw their audience from the local community only.

Some festivals are concerned with only one art form. Many include activities in many different art forms. In addition to almost every type of music, there are festivals of dance, drama, film, literature, poetry and puppetry and a number offering innovative combinations of art forms. Indeed, the diversity of festivals is so great that there is more than a grain of truth in one festival organiser's comment that the only thing they have in common is the 'festival' title. However, this would be to ignore the characteristic that they share – an intensity of artistic output and experience that can be achieved by a programme which is concentrated in time and delivered with a clear purpose and direction.

Although many are small-scale, taken together arts festivals are big business. Box office income at arts festivals in 1991 amounted to an estimated total of £17.6 million. Funding from local authorities or local arts associations amounted to an estimated total of £7 million and income from regional arts boards amounted to an estimated £2 million. Festivals have increasingly attracted business sponsorship. In 1991 they received an estimated £6.8 million in sponsorship (see Appendix 2).

Methods of the study

The postal survey

The purpose of this study is to provide a reasonably comprehensive account of the artistic programmes, organisation and economics of arts festivals, and thereby to fill a gap in knowledge of cultural activity. Most of the data was collected through a postal survey which was completed by 66% of the 527 arts festivals that were defined as eligible. Included in the survey were all festivals that are held regularly, that are more than one day in duration, that are not wholly competitive or held for children only, and that have some professional input on the organisational or artistic side. It was felt necessary to exclude from the survey 'festivals' which would more appropriately be termed 'seasons' in that they are part of the regular programme of concert halls or other arts venues and lack the intensity of programming characteristic of arts festivals. However, the Henry Wood Promenade Concerts and the Bristol Proms are included because they are concentrated in time. The questionnaire asked for information on festival activities and programme, organisation and staffing, audiences and attendances and finances (for questionnaires see Appendix 1). The questionnaires were first issued in November 1991 and returns were analysed in February and March 1992. For a breakdown of responses by festival type see Table 1.

On a number of measures, including size and income, a few large festivals outweigh the majority of smaller ones many times over. Therefore, where an average is presented, this has been selected as the median or mid-point. The more commonly adopted statistical measure, the mean, the sum of the total divided by the number of cases, would be disproportionately influenced by the larger festivals. For the same reason, where data are grossed up to calculate a total figure, for ticket sales and total income for example, the smaller festivals have been given a higher weighting so that the larger ones do not artificially inflate the total (see Appendix 2). With the exception of these

Table 1   **Festivals responding to the survey**

Type of festival	Number	% of total
General arts	138	40
Mixed music	29	8
Classical music	36	10
Jazz	31	9
Folk	70	20
Literature	9	3
Film	8	2
Other single art form	28	8

estimates, all other statistics given in the report refer to the 349 festivals which responded to the survey.

Regional distribution

The festivals that we defined as eligible for the survey show an uneven geographical distribution. Analysis of the location of festivals by countyy and regional arts boards (RAB) shows Scotland (where there are no RABs) having the largest number. Its 63 festivals account for 12% of the total. Table 2 gives the number of festivals per country and region and the number of festivals by population. For the UK as a whole, there are 8 arts festivals for every million people.

An additional analysis was carried out of the response rate of festivals according to region. This found the response rate to be representative of the regional distribution, with the exception of the West Midlands where the proportion of folk festivals responding to our survey was lower than the proportion accounted for by that region.

Folk festivals

Of the 527 festivals invited to take part in the survey, 105 covered folk arts only. These folk festivals are usually held over the course of a weekend and tend to have a higher degree of voluntary involvement on the organisational side than arts festivals in general. A separate questionnaire was designed for these festivals, although many of the questions to the general arts festivals questionnaire were included. Indeed, the majority of analyses in this report include data from both

Table 2 **Number of festivals per head of population, by country and English region**

Region and country	Number of festivals in region/country	Festivals per million population
East Anglia	52	25
East Midlands	10	2
London	44	6
North	34	11
North West	28	4
South and South East*	94	5
South West	51	11
West Midlands	49	9
Yorkshire & Humberside	35	7
Scotland	63	12
Northern Ireland	21	13
Wales	46	16
Total	527	8

* The figures in this line combine those for the areas covered by the two regional arts boards of South and South East England.

arts and folk festivals, the latter constituting 20% of our sample. Where we refer to 'arts festivals' this should be taken to include folk festivals. Where data do not include folk festivals, or where we have carried out separate analyses by festival type, this is made explicit in the text.

Interviews with festival organisers

In addition to the postal survey, structured interviews were carried out with 16 festival directors, managers or organisers. The purpose of this exercise was to put the findings of the survey into a broader context and to explore issues of importance to arts festivals in a way that is not possible in a postal survey. Festivals were selected to include a range by geographical area and by festival type. They include 5 general arts festivals: the Edinburgh International Festival, the Bradford Festival, the Bury St Edmunds Festival, the Swansea Festival and Gwyl Llanelli Festival; 3 classical or mixed music festivals: the

Aldeburgh Festival, the Harrogate Festival and Bristol Proms; 2 folk festivals: the Sidmouth Festival of International Folk Arts and the Warwick Folk Festival, along with the Notting Hill Carnival, the Camden Jazz Festival, the London Film Festival, the Edinburgh Fringe Festival, 'Vision Mix' – a festival of puppetry and its links with film, television and video – and the Essex Festival – a literature festival.

Thirteen of these festivals are run by paid staff, of whom 6 are employed by local authorities and 1 is based in an arts centre. The remaining 3 festivals are run by volunteers and, of these, one is an arts festival, one a folk festival and the other a literature festival. Issues covered in the interviews included the artistic and social aspirations of festivals; their criteria and methods of planning programmes; their systems of evaluation; their priorities and needs for development; their experiences of seeking financial and other support from arts organisations, local authorities and business; their audiences and the balance between professional and amateur involvement. Interviews were carried out between November 1991 and January 1992.

The importance of arts festivals

The study was designed to establish a picture of arts festivals in the United Kingdom, which will inform policy makers and the arts community about the economic and artistic importance of festivals. Combining the two methods of postal questionnaire and structured interview allowed for statistical information to be supported with some in-depth qualitative data on particular festivals and the opinions and experiences of their directors and other key personnel.

Detailed information of both types is necessary to develop policy in this important area, but we would not wish to suggest that we are alone in undertaking to this task. The formation of a National Arts and Media Strategy has included an examination of the role and importance of arts festivals (Curtis and Henderson, 1991) and closer links with mainland Europe, as we approach the completion of the Single European Market, have led to some comparisons between the status and funding of festivals in other European countries with those in the UK. Aspects of the festival style and format have been adopted in a number of national initiatives: the Prime Minister, John Major, has proposed staging a national arts festival during his period of presidency of the European Council of Ministers, the Arts Council is promoting the idea of year-long festivals under its Arts 2000 scheme, and the former Arts Minister, Timothy Renton, formed a partnership with Mick Jagger to promote National Music Day on 28 June 1992. These initiatives reflect a growing recognition of the capacity of arts festivals to act as high points in the cultural calendar.

In addition to their artistic and cultural importance, arts festivals have considerable economic value, which is demonstrated in this report. This has a number of aspects: the arts are a source of direct employment and a generator of growth in ancillary industries; audiences for festivals increase the demand for retail, catering, accommodation and transport services and are a particular stimulus to the tourist and leisure industry (see Myerscough et al., 1988). Festivals can also assist in promoting economic regeneration by adding to the social vitality and attractiveness of a region and boosting the pride and self-confidence of its people. These are particularly important considerations, given the increasing importance of the service sector to the UK economy.

The report

The report presents the findings of the postal survey, representing 349 arts festivals, and in-depth interviews with 16 festival organisers. Chapter 1 examines the historical development of arts festivals and the characteristics of arts festivals in the UK, including their origins, duration and frequency. It also looks at their objectives and constitutional arrangements. Chapter 2 examines the festival programme and includes an analysis of which art forms predominate at festivals. It looks at how decisions are made on the artistic programme, including the role of new commissions, the use of themes and the educational content. Data on festival artists are presented, including the balance of professionals and amateurs. Chapter 3 looks in detail at the festival audience, including its estimated size and type and at the factors which influence audiences and attendances. Chapter 4 covers the staffing of festivals, including the basis on which paid staff are employed and the role of volunteers. Chapter 5 looks at questions of funding, including sources of income, areas of expenditure and the implications of current funding arrangements for the fulfilment of festivals' objectives. Chapter 6 explores the future of arts festivals, their direction and the developments and issues which they see as most important to their survival and growth.

1 Arts Festivals in the UK: Background and Objectives

Introduction: the origins and development of arts festivals

Arts festivals, defined in the broadest sense, have been held for many hundreds of years. A festival was traditionally a time of celebration, relaxation and recuperation which often followed a period of hard physical labour, sowing or harvesting of crops, for example. The essential feature of these festivals was the celebration or reaffirmation of community or culture. The artistic content of such events was variable and many had a religious or ritualistic aspect, but music, dance and drama were important features of the celebration.

The majority of arts festivals, however, while they may share some of the features of the traditional community-based festival in seeing it as a period of intense artistic activity, have different origins and objectives. The oldest festivals included in our study are Scarborough Fayre, first held in 1161, and the Three Choirs Festival, first held in 1713. Only 6 festivals in our study predate the twentieth century and only 5% of our total were first held before the end of World War Two. The oldest festivals include the Norfolk and Norwich Festival (1789), the Royal National Eisteddfod of Wales (revived in 1880), the Mary Wakefield Westmorland Festival (1885) and the BBC Henry Wood Promenade Concerts (1895) which predate their host institution by some years. Of the folk festivals in our study, only 2 were first held before 1960: the Gloucester Carnival Festival (1945) and the Sidmouth Festival of International Folk Arts (1955). The pre-1945 festivals are largely musical events rather than general arts festivals, which are a more modern phenomenon.

Some of the more prominent festivals were created by arts practitioners who saw the arts as a means of promoting contact between European countries, following the destruction brought about by two world wars. Festivals including Edinburgh, Aldeburgh,

Table 3   Year of origin of arts festivals

	% of total
Pre 1940	4
1940s	4
1950s	3
1960s	12
1970s	21
1980s	51
1990s*	5

*   1990 and 1991 only

Swansea, Cheltenham and Bath flourished in this period of optimism and artistic endeavour, although this European dimension varies. Classical music forms the major part of their programmes, with orchestral performances featured as the key attraction. Despite the reputation and influence of this group of festivals, only 7% of festivals in our survey date from the 1940s and 1950s.

The number of arts festivals increased steadily during the 1960s and 1970s with several of the larger ones receiving fairly substantial Arts Council support. But only a minority of festivals in the study were established before 1980. Table 3 shows the distribution by decade of origin. There was a real expansion in this area of cultural activity during the 1980s. The observed success of the well-established festivals in attracting audiences, public funding and, increasingly, business sponsorship, was a source of encouragement to arts enthusiasts working independently, but also to local authorities and arts centres in many towns and cities. Another important impetus was the proven benefit of festivals in attracting tourists to an area, particularly where venues were sufficiently impressive to create a festive atmosphere with relative ease. As a recent article in *Classical Music* (4 May 1991) observes, for most festival cities the initial attraction was the generation of extra income during the traditionally lean cultural period of the school holidays, which is also the tourist season.

The development of the regional arts associations in the 1970s and 1980s and the promotion of links with local authorities led to a new emphasis on support for community activities. Some local authorities recognised the role of the arts in regeneration through the promotion of tourism in areas which had suffered the decline of their traditional industries.

Bradford is an example of one of the most innovative and successful festivals of this type. A number of the festivals which resulted from this shift in policy drew upon a range of artistic forms and traditions and in some cases explicitly recognised and incorporated other, non-European, cultures represented in local communities. Some of these festivals included a processional component or similar outdoor participatory events.

Other festivals which grew in the new atmosphere of the mid to late 1980s were more directly the result of artistic developments. Gavin Henderson refers (Curtis and Henderson, 1991) to these festivals as a 'second generation' of post-war festivals. Their aims were to promote contemporary work and 'their justification was based on the collective strength a festival could bring the emergent artists and ideas'. Festivals with this impetus include the Brighton International Festival and the Huddersfield Festival of Contemporary Music. A substantial proportion of the new festivals presented single art forms, including drama, dance and literature.

Survey data suggest that the proliferation of festivals is a recent phenomenon, dating from the mid 1970s. However, a more pessimistic interpretation could be placed on our figures, namely, the short life of many arts festivals. Our survey includes festivals currently in existence and we have no data on the number of festivals which have ceased to exist. Several that were contacted are no longer organised and a number reported that their 1991 festival would in all probability be their last. This suggests some turnover in festivals. However, it is generally agreed that the 1980s was a period of quite remarkable growth for arts festivals, and the issue of most interest is the long-term prospects for these as well as for the more established festivals. This issue is considered in later chapters of this report.

The variety of arts festivals

Table 1 in the Introduction to this report shows the respondents to the survey by type of festival. The largest single group is general arts festivals which cover a range of art forms, including music of various types, drama and film (see Chapter 2 for a typical profile of a general arts festival). The second largest group is folk festivals, which form 20% of the total, followed by festivals covering a single art form, such as dance, film, drama, literature, and international music.

It was suggested above that the earliest festivals were community celebrations with a variable artistic content. Many festivals include activities for adults other than arts events, performances and exhibitions. These include talks and competitions as well as a wide variety of other social and recreational activities. The importance of such activities to folk festivals is well-known, but survey data shows half of all arts festivals (excluding folk), include non-arts activities. In most cases, the proportion of arts activities is still high: in only 35% of arts festivals is the proportion of non-arts activities greater than 10% and in only 5% of arts festivals is it greater than 30%.

The great majority (91%) of festivals take place on an annual basis: only 7% are held every other year and the remainder either twice a year or at intervals of several years. The most usual length of a festival is between 8 and 14 days: 34% are of this length, 26% between 2 and 3 days and 18 percent between 4 and 7 days; 22% are more than 2 weeks but less than a month long. Only a tiny minority fit none of these time periods and are either more than a month long or held over a series of weekends with no weekday events. Table 4 shows the duration of festivals by festival type.

Table 4 Duration of festivals, by festival type

Percentages

Type of festival	Duration: 2-3 days	4-7 days	8-14 days	2 weeks-1 month	Total	Total respondents by type
General arts	6	13	49	32	100	138
Mixed music	11	31	31	27	100	29
Classical music	11	36	34	19	100	36
Jazz	42	23	32	3	100	31
Folk	76	17	4	3	100	70
Single art form	22	13	36	29	100	45
Total	26	18	34	22	100	
No	92	64	118	75		349

Table 5 Festivals by month held

Percentages

	General arts	Mixed music	Classical music	Jazz	Folk	Single art form
January	0	0	0	3	1	2
February	1	0	0	0	0	4
March	1	7	3	3	3	7
April	2	3	6	0	7	7
May	20	10	28	10	23	9
June	17	10	17	23	17	7
July	25	31	19	16	13	9
August	13	7	17	26	21	18
September	6	14	6	13	9	9
October	10	10	6	3	4	18
November	2	3	0	3	4	11
December	0	0	0	0	0	0
Not given	1	3	0	0	0	0
Total	100	100	100	100	100	100

*   Some columns do not total 100 because of rounding.

The attraction of festivals in the generation of additional income for arts venues in the school summer holidays and their role in attracting tourists to an area was referred to earlier, as was the importance of outdoor events to some festivals. July is the most popular month for festivals (see Table 5): 20% are held during that month. The second most popular month is May (18%), followed by August and June (16%); all but 9% of the rest take place during September, October and November. Very few festivals take place between January and April and, to our knowledge, none are held during December.

Folk festivals show an even greater degree of concentration in the summer months, with 74% taking place from May to August. The proliferation of folk festivals in May and August is partly accounted for by the Bank Holidays in these months.

The diverse origins and characteristics of arts festivals have resulted in wide variations in their forms of organisation and constitution. Constitutional arrangements are complex and many do not fit easily into a choice of categories. Nearly 40% have a festival committee, 28% are companies limited by guarantee and 17% are the direct responsibility of local authorities. However, this figure certainly understates the involvement of local authorities. Other festivals have substantial local authority support, in terms of funding and staff; 75% receive income from local authorities and 53% receive support in kind, but have the status of an ad-hoc festival committee, a trust, a company limited by guarantee or other status. A number of festivals are run by a host institution.

It was suggested earlier that the availability of a suitable venue, often a beautiful concert hall or church, has helped motivate the organisers of some festivals. We also referred to the role of arts centres in staging festivals. An earlier PSI study (Hutchison and Forester, 1987) found that half of the arts centres in the UK organised a festival in 1985-6, of which roughly half were based on a single art form. 30% of respondents to the survey were venue-based and classical music festivals are more likely than others to be in this group. Mixed music festivals are also more likely to take place largely or entirely at a single venue, while general arts festivals are least likely to be in this situation.

Festival objectives

Arts festivals share the general objectives of staging events and performances of a high standard, concentrated in a relatively short period of time, but their particular objectives can differ widely. The relationship between festivals and year-round activity is varied, but in many cases the festival is seen as the culmination of a year-round programme and includes events and performances which would not otherwise have taken place.

Following his visit to the first Aldeburgh Festival in 1948 E.M. Forster remarked in a BBC radio broadcast that 'A festival should be festive. And it should possess something which is distinctive and which could not be so well presented elsewhere' (Aldeburgh Foundation, 1987). The Aldeburgh Festival was one of a group which grew in the atmosphere of regeneration following the Second World War, and had a particular set of objectives which included presenting new work. The festivals established during this period saw their role as promoting the arts to encourage international friendship between artists and arts enthusiasts. A more concrete aim of some festivals was to increase the accessibility and affordability of the arts.

Numerous festivals were established with the principal objective of presenting professional arts of a standard and scale which is not possible to sustain all the year round. Indeed, the original impetus of many festivals came from local people who felt the absence of high quality artistic events and performances in their area and saw a festival as a means of attracting performers. Most of these festivals aimed to cater primarily for the local community, although some succeeded in attracting tourists. At the same time, festivals have been created with a tourist audience in mind, and 56% of all festivals aim to attract tourists. However, in some cases the stimulus to the tourist industry has been used as a means of persuading a local authority to provide funding. Paradoxically, among the festivals which have succeeded in attracting tourists are some that did not have this as a principal aim.

A festival can provide a 'focus' for the arts which can encourage attendance and involvement throughout the year; some festivals are aimed specifically at promoting attendance at arts events other than the festival itself. The Bristol Proms is an example of this type. Other festivals are held more with the aim of compensating for, or boosting, artistic activity, particularly where absence of a large, purpose-built, venue restricts a year-round programme. The arts festival in Bury St Edmunds is an example of a festival with this aim.

In some cases audiences are not sufficiently large for performances by large national orchestras to be financially viable, but a festival umbrella can attract a bigger audience that makes it possible to stage more expensive events. A festival is therefore seen in some cases as an opportunity to give local people access to events and artistic experiences which would otherwise not be possible. More generally, festivals provide opportunities to raise the profile of a particular type of music or other art form.

A festival has traditionally been a time of celebration and rejuvenation for a community, and a large proportion of contemporary festivals have retained this as part of their identity, defining their community in various ways. Some festivals have a focus on regional or national cultural identities and this is particularly true of festivals in Wales and Scotland: for example, one of the policy objectives of the Edinburgh International Festival is to foster Scottish culture and its international recognition. A number of festivals have tried principally to revive or sustain traditional local culture and cultural practices and have seen support for local artists as an important means of achieving this aim. A smaller number have explicitly acknowledged the cultural transformation of their communities and have seen the festival format as a means of celebrating the multi-cultural nature of many (particularly urban) communities. Other festivals adopt similar celebratory aspects, in that they aim to present a range of traditional and contemporary cultures in their artistic input, but with no particular geographical focus. A number of folk festivals may be included in this group, although their emphasis tends to be on sustaining traditional cultural forms.

There is also an emerging group emphasising contemporary arts, including dance, film and international, world, music. Particularly interesting here is the success of this group in attracting a young and participatory audience, which has been an unfulfilled goal of many of the larger arts and folk festivals.

Key points

- Despite their diverse origins, festivals share the basic objective of staging performances and events of a high standard, concentrated in a short period of time. Their broader objectives differ widely, as does the relationship between festivals and year-round activity in the places in which they are organised.

- The end of the Second World War saw the birth of some of the larger and more prestigious music festivals, although they represent a small proportion of all arts festivals.

- The majority of arts festivals were established during the 1980s.

- Local authorities have been an important force behind the development of arts festivals, with tourism and local economic development major considerations behind local authority support.

- Festivals covering a range of art forms – general arts festivals – are the largest single group of festivals, representing 39% of the total.

- Half of all arts festivals (excluding folk) include non-arts activities.

- Most festivals take place on an annual basis. July is the most popular month and the most usual length of a festival is between 8 and 14 days. Folk and jazz festivals are more likely than other festivals to be held over a 2-3 day period.

- 30% of festivals are venue-based. Classical music festivals are more likely than other types of festival to be based in one venue.

2   The Festival Programme and Festival Artists

Introduction: the festival programme

The shared objective of arts festivals to create a concentrated period of artistic activity is realised either by focusing on a single, or limited, group of art forms, or by embracing a variety of arts in a general celebration. The median number of art forms covered by arts festivals is 6, but this figure is distorted by the number of festivals which cover a single art form. The median number of art forms covered by general arts festivals is 10.

Analysis of the survey data for arts festivals (excluding folk festivals) shows orchestral, choral, chamber/soloist and jazz as the art forms most likely to be included; half of all arts festivals included

Table 6   Festivals' coverage of art forms

In half of all festivals(%)	In between a third and a half of all festivals(%)	In between a quarter and a third of all festivals(%)	In fewer than a quarter of all festivals(%)
Jazz (53)	Orchestral (49)	Cabaret/comedy (30)	Rock/pop (23)
Choral (50)	Visual arts (42)	Folk* (29)	Opera (21)
Chamber/ soloist (54)	Drama (40)	Film (26)	Contemporary dance (19)
	Literature (36)	Craft (26)	Puppetry (18)
		Folk/ethnic dance (25)	Carnival (17)
			Musicals/ light opera (14)
			Classical ballet (10)
			Mime (9)

*   also in over 100 folk festivals

performances in at least one of these categories in their most recent festival. Other popular programme choices, included by more than a third of festivals, were drama, visual arts, and literature. Table 6 shows the frequency with which particular art forms are included in festival programmes.

On average, a general arts festival will include about 24 performances or events. The following art forms were included in the most recent programmes of over half of all general arts festivals: drama, visual arts, orchestral, chamber/soloist, choral, jazz, literature/poetry, folk, other music, cabaret/comedy. Table 7 shows the median number of performances and art forms covered by other types of festival. There is no definite relationship between the size of festival, as measured in the number of events, and festival income, which suggests that the larger festivals may stage more expensive events rather than a greater number of events than the smaller festivals.

Table 7   Arts festivals and performances/events by festival type

Type of festival	Average number of art forms	Average number of performances/events
General arts	10	24
Mixed music	5	12
Classical	3	10
Single art form	2	45

A substantial majority include a range of art forms. Even in the case of the art forms included in a relatively small proportion of festivals, survey data suggest that they are included in festivals other than those that concentrate on one art form. For example, film festivals are only 3% of festivals (excluding folk) yet film is included in 26% of festivals; jazz festivals are only 11% of the total yet jazz is included in 53% of festivals; drama festivals are only 1% of the total, yet drama is included in 40% of festivals; and, although there were only 2 festivals in our survey dedicated exclusively to the visual arts – the Cleveland Visual Arts Festival and Artweek, Oxfordshire – the visual arts are included in 42% of all festivals.

Festivals also include other types of music, dance and other arts events than those listed above. 40% include other types of music, principally ethnic and world music, brass bands, country and western and blues: 12% include forms of dance other than classical, contemporary and folk/ethnic; these are principally jazz dance, ballroom and tea dancing, and morris dancing, which is often an important ingredient in folk festivals.

Festival art forms

It was noted above that 4 art forms are included in at least half of all festivals (excluding folk festivals): jazz, choral, chamber/soloist and orchestral music. The average number of performances shows considerable variation by art form. For example, a carnival is usually a single event, while almost half of all festivals which included chamber/soloist works had more than 6 or more such performances in their 1991 programme. Some art forms, for example, film, literature and jazz, are included in the programmes of general arts festivals and in those festivals which focus on one art form. However, even these festivals frequently include several art forms: for example, drama and literature festivals often include musical events in addition to their main programme.

This section of the report summarises the place of the 4 major art forms – jazz, choral, chamber/soloist and orchestral, to festival programmes and, in addition, highlights the principal characteristics of the largest groupings of single art form festivals. The section also summarises the place of some of the performing art forms – drama, mime, and cabaret/comedy – which appear in a minority of arts festivals.

Orchestral, choral, and chamber/soloist performances

Orchestral performances are often a festival's main highlight and the means of attracting a large audience. The number of such performances is usually small: only 5 festivals staged more than 20 orchestral performances. These included the National Festival of Music for Youth (25 performances), the Festival of British Youth Orchestras in Edinburgh (30 performances) and the Edinburgh Festival Fringe (81 orchestral performances).

Half of all festivals included choral works in their 1991 programme and the majority of these staged between 1 and 3 such performances. The Llangollen International Musical Eisteddfod (170 performances) accounted for 27% of all performances in this category.

The majority of festivals which included chamber or soloist performances in their 1991 programme staged between 1 and 5 performances; but 11% staged more than 21 performances. Again, the Llangollen Musical Eisteddfod, which included 275 performances by soloists, accounted for a substantial proportion of all festival performances in this category.

Jazz performances and jazz festivals

The majority of arts festivals included jazz in their most recent festival programme. Most of these had between 1 and 3 jazz events, and interview data suggest that the addition of a jazz event is a fairly recent development for many festivals, and is partly aimed at attracting a wider and younger audience. Festivals devoted specifically to jazz are also of recent origin: all but 2 of the 31 jazz festivals in the survey were first held in the 1980s or 1990s (see Table 8).

Table 8   Year of origin of jazz festivals

	Number of festivals
1940s	–
1950s	–
1960s	–
1970s	2
1980s	23
1990s	5

Literature events and literature festivals

36% of all festivals (excluding folk festivals) included literature or poetry events in their most recent festival. 9 literature festivals responded to the survey questionnaire. Of these, the Edinburgh Book Festival included 194 literary events and over 170 non-literary events. The Birmingham Readers and Writers Festival included 200 literary events. Other large literature festivals include the Cheltenham Festival of Literature (58 events), and the Cardiff Literature Festival (38 events).

Table 9 Number of performances and events at literature and film festivals

	Literature festivals	Film festivals
1-10	1	–
11-20	–	1
21-40	3	–
41-70	2	1
71-100	–	1
100+	2	3

The number of events and performances given at literature festivals is shown in Table 9. Literature festivals frequently include other art forms. For example, the Birmingham Readers and Writers Festival includes performances and events in drama, cabaret/comedy, film and visual arts, and the Edinburgh Book Festival includes puppetry performances and craft events.

Film screenings and film festivals
26% of festivals included film screenings in their most recent festival. Interview data suggest that film is increasingly included in programmes to attract a wider audience. Festivals include film to a varying extent, as shown in Table 9. Only 4 (all film festivals) included more than 100 film screenings. These were International Animation (500 screenings), the Birmingham International Film and Television Festival (200 screenings), the London Film Festival (220 screenings), and the Edinburgh International Film Festival (380 screenings).

Drama, mime, cabaret and comedy
Festivals are an opportunity to give exposure to art forms which tend not to attract widespread interest and high audiences in all-year-round programmes. Mime is one such example. The purpose of the London Mime Festival is stated by its organisers as 'to make a concerted push on behalf of the art form once a year... It is still largely a difficult art form to promote outside the festival.' Its 1991 festival included 69 performances. Of the 9% of festivals which included mime, only 2 others staged more than 8 mime performances: the Cardiff Summer

Festival (30 performances) and the Edinburgh Festival Fringe (37 performances).

Drama is included in the programmes of 40% of all festivals. 3 drama festivals responded to the survey: the London International Festival of Theatre, which staged 24 drama events and, in addition, puppetry, carnival, visual arts and contemporary dance; the National Student Drama Festival, which staged 32 drama performances, 60 workshops and 7 discussions; and the Minack Theatre Summer Festival in Cornwall (77 drama and 37 opera, light opera and choral performances).

It was clear from the interviews conducted that arts festivals are including more and more cabaret and comedy in their programmes because of their popularity among young people, a target group for many festivals. Only 1 festival in the survey was a comedy festival, the Liverpool Festival of Comedy. It held 250 events including cabaret/comedy, carnival, jazz, folk, pop, film, literature and a 'surrealist bus tour' with George Melly. The organisers of the Edinburgh Festival Fringe estimate that there were 2,500 cabaret and comedy performances in the 1991 festival. However, the majority of festivals which included cabaret and comedy did so on a far more limited scale.

Folk festivals and folk performances

70 folk festivals responded to the survey, and these respondents reported having organised a total of 4,400 performances and events at their most recent festivals. The special nature of folk festivals has already been noted in this report: 76% of folk festivals are 2 or 3 day events, compared to 26% of all festivals; and folk festivals are more highly concentrated in the summer months than other festivals. They have other features which give them a celebratory character: although concentrated in time, they include a higher median number of performances than any other type of festival; with the exception of festivals covering a single art form, they have smaller audiences than other types of festival; and only a small minority adopt an annual theme (see below and Table 11). They often include larger numbers of amateur artists and are more likely than other festivals to be organised by volunteers (see Chapter 4).

Fringe festivals

The Edinburgh Festival Fringe is the largest festival in the UK. The 1991 festival included over 9,000 fringe events, sold over half a million tickets and had a total income of over £500,000. There are a number of other fringe festivals in the UK established on a similar basis to the Edinburgh Festival Fringe, to allow open access to performers rather than operating on a basis of selection and invitation. The number of fringe festivals in our study (3) is too small to draw any conclusions on programme content, or any other feature. However, we found that of all festivals (excluding folk), 20% had a fringe festival. Mixed music festivals are more likely than other types to have an 'organised' fringe.

Children's events

Many festival organisers are concerned to involve all sections of the population and the local community in festival events (see Chapter 3). Children are one such group and the benefits of providing entertainment can be experienced in higher attendances from parents who see interest for their children and for themselves in a festival programme. Later in the report we look at festivals' priorities for development which include, in some cases, plans to increase festival attendances by children and young people and to nurture a future adult audience.

The majority of festivals (including folk festivals) include a special programme of events for children. 63% of festivals make provision for children, but in most cases the number of events is fewer than 10. Those most likely to include children's events are general arts festivals (76%) and folk festivals (86%). Only 25% of classical music festivals and 35% of jazz festivals included events for children in their most recent programmes. 23% of festivals which included children's events organised more than 10 such events and 3 organised over 100 children's events: the Sidmouth International Festival of Folk Arts (120 events), the Aberdeen Arts Carnival (174 events) and the Edinburgh Festival Fringe (528 events).

Educational content

Many festival organisers regard the festival as having a role to play in education. All arts festivals aim to educate their audience in the broadest sense by widening access to arts performances and events.

However, many have taken a closer look at how they might inform and enlighten adult and child audiences by providing an explicitly educational content in their programmes: 56% of festivals (excluding folk) included an explicitly educational component in their most recent festival. General arts and mixed music festivals are more likely than other festivals to include such an element.

Festivals with higher than average levels of public funding (from local authorities, regional arts boards and arts councils) are more likely to carry out educational work than those with lower than average such funding. The median income from public sources of festivals which included an educational component in their most recent festival was £5,775, compared to £2,500 for those without such a component. It would appear that it is income from this source which is of most influence, since the difference in average total incomes of festivals with and without an educational component is only 25%. Levels of business sponsorship may also be a factor, since sponsorship of festivals which include an educational component is, on average, 40% higher than of those which do not (see Table 10).

Table 10   Funding of festivals with an educational component (excluding folk)

	Festivals including educational component	Festivals not including educational component
Average public subsidy (local authorities/regional arts boards/arts councils)	5,775	2,500
Average arts subsidy (regional & national)	725	0
Average total income	32,500	24,545
Average business sponsorship	4,560	2,750

Education within arts festivals takes a variety of forms. Many have developed links with local schools to run educational activities relating to festival events, either in the class-room or as part of the festival itself. In some cases arrangements are made for artists or groups to visit schools to perform or give talks, but the emphasis in educational work for children is on workshops and practical involvement. This ranges from poetry competitions to workshops in circus skills and kite-making. Some festivals integrate educational work closely with their programme by organising performances by children attending workshops. The Melrose Music Festival holds a 3-day instrument workshop for local school children prior to the festival, directed by a group of visiting artists. The festival is formally opened with a procession led by the children playing instruments made in the workshops.

With regard to adult education, festival activity includes holding lectures, pre-performance talks, workshops and master classes. Some festival organisers like to give audiences the opportunity to handle and play the instruments that they see in use during the festival, and this seems to be particularly common in jazz festivals. Folk festivals in the survey were not asked about their educational activities, but interview data suggest a similar orientation. For example, the Sidmouth International Festival of Folk Arts holds workshops throughout the festival, and in 1991 held 250 workshops which were attended by 4,600 people. Many of these were adults taking the opportunity to try their hand at playing instruments, dancing or meeting artists to discuss their work.

The emphasis of adult educational work is on increasing participation and access and enhancing the festive atmosphere. This is also a consideration in educational work with children, but there is an additional purpose here in the need to nurture a future arts audience and fresh artistic talent. This has sometimes involved staging events with a younger appeal, through a fringe festival for example, although fringe events are usually aimed at an older, student, audience rather than at school-age children.

Many festival organisers are aware that their audiences are aging and feel an urgent need to attract a new and younger audience. They therefore regard the expansion of educational work as a priority. The report published in 1992 by the Scottish Tourist Board on the Edinburgh Festivals identifies a need for greater resources to be put behind attracting young people to the festivals, either in school parties or as individuals. Some festivals have created education or community officer posts, to visit schools and youth groups to encourage projects which are complementary to the festival or to build links in other ways. The availability of local authority support for such work has been important in some cases. Some festivals are also able to assist schools with particular courses. For example, the London Film Festival is able to complement courses in film and media by creating opportunities for school and college students to discuss film content and the process of film-making.

Some festivals encourage schools to make block bookings for performances. There is an increasing emphasis, however, on educating children in the school environment so that festivals have arranged for artists to visit schools to present and discuss their work. The availability of funding for this work is patchy and, in addition, some festival organisers feel unable to develop it because their festival takes place during school holidays – a traditional period for festivals. Other festivals have found ways of organising educational work with school children in the school holidays, although the need remains for financial resources being available either in the school's budget, or for the festival itself. A number of festival organisers expressed concern at what they saw as inadequate support from central government in this area.

Two examples of imaginative work in the field of education are provided by the Bury St Edmunds and Bradford Festivals. The Bury St Edmunds Festival includes workshops for children in percussion and puppet-making, and each year it runs separate projects for children at upper, middle and primary schools. The 1992 festival planned to focus its educational work on music for film and to involve the upper schools in composition and the middle and primary schools in 'sounds' projects based on the science national curriculum, involving a BBC engineer and a percussionist.

The involvement of the Bradford Festival began with a touring puppet show and now includes the staging of an opera with pupils from 7 local schools. The education programme also includes a number of one-off performances in schools and projects of several months duration, involving professional artists with project work in schools. The festival organisers are currently planning a competition among schools to design a festival stage. The process will include art, technology and design, physics, mathematics, engineering and accounting and will be tailored to the national curriculum.

Decisions on the artistic programme

In 47% of festivals (excluding folk festivals) decisions on the main artistic programme are made by the festival director, and in 45% of cases by the festival committee. In some festivals where decisions are made by a festival director, a committee will be involved to some extent. Where a festival has a constitution involving a committee, decisions on the artistic programme are more likely to be made on this basis: in 62% of festivals with a committee constitution, decisions on the programme are made by a committee.

Although festival directors are responsible for making decisions on the festival programme in a substantial proportion of cases, their degree of autonomy varies widely and our interview data suggest that complete autonomy or overriding influence is unusual. This is perhaps the result of the involvement of local authorities, which often require a democratic structure of decision-making. However, the festival committee's control over programme content may be limited in some cases by their knowledge of artistic developments and the availability of performers. In many cases they 'rubber stamp' the decisions of a director and his or her team. However, some committees are highly structured and include much collaborative decision-making. For example, the Llanelli Festival, which is not a local-authority event, has a committee and sub-committees for particular aspects of the programme. The Bradford Festival engages in an even greater degree of public consultation, contacting over 400 community groups during the year to ask what they would like to contribute to the festival. Some of these groups are able to suggest international artists, thereby acting as unofficial artistic advisers. The programme of the Edinburgh Fringe is decided directly by the artists and groups who wish to perform at the festival, and none appear by invitation.

A number of large festivals employ a small team of artistic directors, who are experts in their field, to advise on particular parts of the programme. For example, decisions on the Aldeburgh Festival programme are made using the combined judgement of the two artistic directors, the Aldeburgh Foundation, the General Director and the Britten trustees. Similarly, the artistic director of the Sidmouth Folk Festival is assisted by a team of advisers with knowledge of particular art forms in different regions of the country.

Smaller festivals are frequently organised by the combined efforts of a small group of local arts enthusiasts working in a voluntary capacity. Decisions are therefore made by fewer than a handful of individuals, often the same people who founded the festival. The Essex Festival and the Warwick Folk Festival are both organised in this way, by two or three enthusiasts who aim to keep continuously abreast of developments in their respective fields, and for whom the festival is an all-year-round concern.

The principal factors taken into account when programmes are drawn up are the budget, the type of audience, its potential size, and the availability of performers. Clearly, in its first year or two, a festival's content and general orientation are the result of initial decisions by its founding members. These include considerations of purpose, which we raised earlier, and of audience, which we examine later. Most festivals develop a basic format consisting of 'slots' which are filled by particular types of performance or event. For example, a general arts festival will typically have a certain number of orchestral concerts, choral and chamber performances and additional events, including a jazz evening and film nights. A festival format may be developed over a number of years as particular types of event are staged at certain times and found to be successful. A number of festivals have a good relationship with particular orchestras or other groups of artists who regularly perform at the festival, and this directly influences the programme. At the same time, it is important to many festivals that the programme has a distinct character and flavour each year.

For most festivals the availability of artists is a central consideration in making decisions on the programme, and here financial considerations also play a crucial role. Sometimes artists will initiate contacts with a festival. It is unusual for a festival to be able to engage an international artist unless he or she is planning a tour of the UK during the festival period, and it is even more unusual for a festival to be able to request a particular piece of an artist or company, since a season's repertoire is usually planned long in advance. Festivals therefore risk the possibility of offering similar programmes to one another.

A well-known artist may well attract a large audience and many festivals therefore aim to feature one or more big names. At the same time, the balance of the programme is important to its overall coherence and appeal. Some festival organisers are concerned that this can be jeopardised when 'star' names are featured. Creating a balanced programme is therefore an important tacit skill of the festival director. In the words of the Director of the Bury St Edmunds Festival, 'Much of it is gut reaction, a feeling for the programme and what falls into your lap'. The order in which events are booked and the programme constructed is also a matter of individual choice and involves highly developed skills of organisation and artistic appreciation. Many festival organisers book the most expensive, or major, performances first and decide the remaining programme gradually and according to the budget, as it becomes known. Many festivals have also to take into account particular matters of tradition or policy. These can include achieving a balance in the number of male and female performers, or a strong representation of local performers, which is particularly common in Welsh and Scottish festivals.

Use of themes

20% of festivals have an annual theme. General arts festivals, mixed music festivals and folk festivals are more likely than other types to have an annual theme (see Table 11). Festivals which adopted a theme at their most recent festival were on average slightly larger, in terms of number of performances, than those which did not. In addition, their average total income was almost twice as large.

Table 11   Festivals adopting an annual theme

				Percentages
Type of festival	Did adopt a theme	Did not adopt a theme	Total	N
General arts	28	72	100	138
Mixed music	28	72	100	29
Classical	26	74	100	36
Jazz	25	75	100	31
Folk	4	96	100	70
Single art form	14	86	100	45
Total	20	80	100	45

1991 was the bicentenary year of Mozart's death and many festivals were built around this anniversary. Festivals with a Mozart theme accounted for 15% of all festivals that adopted a theme in that year. One of the most popular choices of theme is a particular country or culture. Some 1991 festivals adopted a European or Eastern European theme and America was also chosen by several festivals. Other choices tend towards the abstract and some examples of these are 'A matter of time' adopted by the Canterbury Festival and 'Flight', chosen by the Flowerfield Festival in Northern Ireland.

Themes are usually adopted with the aim of giving a festival some extra coherence and individual identity. However, there is a danger that a theme might mask, rather than convey, a particular identity and could alienate a potential audience unfamiliar with its particular artistic and cultural reference. Some themes have an instant appeal and interest: 'the environment'; chosen by the Craigmillar Festival in Edinburgh, is one such example.

Many of the festivals which adopt a theme do not make a choice of theme and develop a programme accordingly. It is more usual for a theme to be decided in the course of programming, and even after a programme has been finalised. Some festivals would like to adopt a theme but find they are unable to construct a programme in this manner because the uncertainty of their budget restricts forward planning. An alternative to a single theme is to have a series of 'threads' running throughout the programme, but this requires much skill in planning which, again, is made difficult by financial limitations in many cases. A second alternative is to seek a common identity among the artists rather than the performances. An example of this is Bradford Festival's idea of inviting performers from minority groups with the member states of the European Community, including Algerians from France and Turks from Germany. This won the festival a 'Platform Europe' award from the European Commission.

Commissioning and innovation

One of the traditional purposes of arts festivals has been to commission new work and to provide an opportunity for artists to present new, and sometimes, innovative work. 42% of general arts festivals and 34% of all festivals (excluding folk festivals) commission new work.

Festivals with higher than average levels of public funding are more likely to do so. The average income from public sources of festivals which commissioned new work at their most recent festival was over three and a half times that of those which did not. Their average business sponsorship and average total income is also more

Table 12   **Funding of festivals commissioning new work**

£

	Festivals commissioning new work	Festivals not commissioning new work
Average public subsidy (local authorities/regional arts boards/ arts councils)	9,155	2,500
Average arts subsidy (regional and national)	1,400	100
Average total income	48,370	23,030
Average business sponsorship	6,020	2,750

than twice that of festivals which did not commission new work (see Table 12).

Some of the older festivals, including Aldeburgh, Swansea and Edinburgh, place a strong emphasis on this commissioning role, which they interpret in different ways. The Aldeburgh Festival acts as host to one or two, usually young, composers each year. The Swansea Festival commissions work, usually by Welsh composers, which is performed by the Welsh Symphony Orchestra in collaboration with BBC Wales and assisted by the Welsh Arts Council. The Bury St Edmunds Festival has a composer in residence and commissions an art work for the cover of its festival programme.

Commissioning is costly and many festivals also stage popular events in order to finance this loss-making work. A number of festival organisers said that they would like to increase their involvement with new artists and performers and provide a platform for new work, but that their financial position was not sufficiently secure to do so. Some festivals also feel restricted in the extent to which they can be innovatory in their programme, since any such performance carries a higher risk than staging a known work. However, innovative events have the potential to attract considerable additional interest. A number of festivals see their main area of innovation as lying in the introduction of international works to the UK, and others in combining different art forms, or in looking at new developments. For example, the Essex Festival has held a series of discussions on the theme of 'art and chips', exploring the effect of computer technology on the arts.

The support given by festivals to new artists and to innovation in the arts therefore varies widely and it is apparent that arts festivals would like to make a greater contribution in this area and indeed feel that they should do so. The survey data suggest that the principal factor preventing this is shortage of funding from public sources. The role of festivals in this regard clearly requires further consideration by policy makers.

Festival artists

Professionals

Almost all of the festivals in our survey (93%) feature professional artists but their number varies greatly, ranging from 2 to 5,850. The median number of professional artists included in the most recent programmes is 40. 8% of festivals featured fewer than 10 professional artists at their most recent festivals, while at 3 festivals: the Edinburgh International Festival, the Edinburgh Festival Fringe, and the BBC Henry Wood Promenade Concerts, the number of professional artists was 2,000 or higher. Other festivals featuring large numbers of professional artists include the Brighton International Festival (1,471), the Cheltenham Festival of Music (1,150) and the Swansea Festival (1,740). General arts festivals and jazz festivals include higher than average numbers of professional artists (see Table 13).

Table 13   Festival artists by festival type

Type of festival	Average number of professional artists	Average number of amateur artists
General arts	70	100
Mixed music	27	18
Classical	42	37
Jazz	62	7
Single art form	40	15
Folk	20	85
All festivals	40	60

81% of festivals featured performances which involved only professional artists, although the majority of festivals also included performances involving only amateur performers and including both professional and amateur performers. Only 17% of festivals that included performances by professional artists did not also include performances by amateurs, or amateurs and professionals together, in their programmes. Festivals featuring no amateur performers account for only 14% of all festivals and classical, mixed music and jazz festivals are more likely than others to be solely professional events. However, although such purely professional festivals are a small minority, in over 50% of festivals that include performances featuring only professional artists 75% or more of the programme covers such events. Therefore, where performances featuring professional artists only are included – and this constitutes the majority of festivals – they tend to account for a major part of the events.

Amateurs

The distinction between professional and amateur artists is not clear-cut. Many artists earn a proportion of their income from performing and are neither fully professional nor are they amateurs. As an earlier study by PSI (Hutchison and Feist, 1991) points out, 'rather than a clear amateur/professional divide, there is a complex amateur/professional continuum, or spectrum of ambition, accomplishment and activity'.

The majority of festivals in our survey feature amateur artists, but the proportion is slightly lower than for festivals featuring professional artists: in 1991 82% of festivals included amateur artists, ranging from 3 to over 10,000. The median number of amateurs included in festivals' most recent programmes was 60. Folk and general arts festivals have higher than average numbers of amateur artists (see Table 13) and jazz festivals have lower than average numbers. However, festivals that include amateurs tend to feature higher numbers of artists than those that are mainly professional. Only 6% of festivals featured fewer than 10 amateur artists and a larger number of festivals included 2,000 or more amateur artists than those featuring professionals. Two possible explanations are the performances by amateur choirs, including children, and those by amateur orchestras. The 6 festivals that included over 2,000 amateur artists in 1991 were the Edinburgh Festival of British Youth Orchestras, the BBC Henry

Wood Promenade Concerts (2,120 amateurs), the Royal National Eisteddfod of Wales (6,500 amateurs), the Edinburgh Festival Fringe (7,750 amateurs) the National Festival of Music for Youth (8,000 amateurs) and the Llangollen International Musical Eisteddfod (10,306 amateurs).

66% of festivals include performances featuring only amateur artists, a smaller proportion than those which include performances featuring only professionals. For the majority of festivals which include performances featuring only amateur artists, such events formed 25% or less of all events and 42% of these were folk festivals. General arts and folk festivals are more likely to feature a higher proportion. This therefore suggests that where amateur-only events are included, as they are in most festivals, they form a minor part of the programme.

Collaboration between professional and amateur performers

Many festivals are concerned to bridge the gap or break down the barriers between professional artists and amateurs. Collaboration between amateurs and professionals is a central feature of many arts festivals, sometimes from a concern to involve the local community and to make it their festival, and sometimes to encourage the development and career opportunities of new artists. 60% of arts festivals include events in which professional and amateur artists perform together. In 15% of these festivals all performances in the programme involve professional and amateur collaboration. Folk festivals are over-represented in this group. In 15% of all festivals the proportion of collaborative professional- amateur events was greater than 50%, and almost half of these are folk festivals.

Welsh arts festivals frequently include performances by several local choirs. Fringe festivals include a large amateur component, often including individuals seeking a professional career who see the festival as a launching pad. The Edinburgh Festival Fringe, for example, features an even mix of professional and amateur artists, and professionals and amateurs often share the same stage. Agents attend the festival to 'talent spot' amateur artists. Folk festivals often include amateurs and professionals in the same festival slot: a typical folk performance will include 5 or 6 separate acts, some amateur, some professional. This is partly because the distinction between professional and amateur artists is even less easily drawn in the folk world than elsewhere and also because the number of professional artists is smaller. The Notting Hill Carnival is perhaps the largest festival in which collaboration between amateurs and professionals is a central feature, and indeed it is described by the organisers as the 'essence' of the carnival form. As noted earlier, other festivals have adopted a processional element with the aim of combining art forms and of increasing amateur involvement.

Most festivals feature both professional and amateur artists and, for this reason, the majority of festivals feature artists from the local area as well as from outside. 57% of festivals feature local and non-local artists, while 33% feature artists chiefly from outside the local community. Only 10% feature artists predominantly from the local area, and general arts festivals are over-represented in this group.

The larger, long established arts festivals, with an emphasis on classical music, do not generally organise collaboration between professionals and amateurs. Two exceptions to this are performances by children and the involvement of local choirs, which are usually accompanied by professional musicians. A number of festival organisers are reluctant to increase the involvement of choral societies or other groups of amateurs either from a fear that artistic standards will be lowered, or out of a reluctance to make decisions on the artistic merits of particular groups. One festival organiser explained that it is considerably easier to judge the merits of a professional artist or group with an established reputation and reviews to support it. An additional problem lies in the danger of creating bad feeling among rejected amateur groups, who are often local people and potential members of the festival audience. If access to the performing side is not open, as it is in a fringe festival or carnival for example, amateur performers may need to be selected on a different basis and according to a different procedure from professional performers. It was suggested that local amateur performers should not be chosen by an identifiable individual because he or she might be subject to personal criticism.

| Key points |

- Orchestral, choral, chamber/soloist and jazz are the art forms most often included in arts festivals' programmes.

- A general arts festival includes an average of 24 performances and events, covering 10 art forms which are most likely to be drama, visual arts, orchestral, chamber/soloist, choral, jazz, literature/ poetry, folk, other music and cabaret/comedy.

- 63% of all festivals include performances or events for children, although in most cases the number of such events is less than 10. General arts festivals and folk festivals are the types most likely to include children's events.

- Festivals which include an educational component have higher levels of funding from public sources than festivals which do not.

- The need to nurture a future audience is a central consideration behind festivals' involvement in educational work and in including a children's programme.

- In 57% of festivals, decisions on the main artistic programme are made by a festival director, and in 45% of cases by a festival committee. Some festivals employ a team of directors.

- 20% of festivals adopt an annual theme, and festivals which do so are, on average, slightly larger and have a higher total income than those which do not.

- One of the traditional purposes of festivals has been to commission new work. 34% of arts festivals (excluding folk) commission new work and general arts festivals are more likely to do so than other festivals. Festivals commissioning new work have higher than average levels of public funding.

- Almost all festivals feature professional artists and the median number of such performers included in a festival is 40. 14% of arts festivals featured performances only by professional artists. Classical, mixed music and jazz festivals are more likely than others to be solely professional events.

- The majority of festivals include performances by amateur artists, the median number of amateur artists included being 60.

- Collaboration between amateur and professional artists is a central feature of many festivals. 60% of arts festivals include events in which professional and amateur artists perform together.

3   The Festival Audience

Ticket sales and attendances at free events

In 1991 festivals sold an estimated total of 4.2 million tickets and box office takings were an estimated £17.6 million. The smallest number of tickets sold was 90 and the festival selling the highest number was the Edinburgh Festival Fringe which sold over half a million tickets. Other festivals with high ticket sales are shown in Table 14 and the distribution of festivals by ticket sales is shown in Table 15. The median number of tickets sold is 2,000. General arts festivals and festivals covering single art forms achieve higher-than-average sales, while the average folk festival sells a smaller number of tickets than other types (see Table 16).

Table 14   Festivals with ticket sales over 100,000 (1991)

Festival	Tickets sold
Edinburgh Festival Fringe	520,000
BBC Henry Wood Promenade Concerts	250,000
Edinburgh International Festival	167,000
Royal National Eisteddfod of Wales	164,000
Brighton International Festival	130,000
Llangollen International Musical Eisteddfod	117,000

Table 15   Distribution of festival ticket sales

Percentages

1-999	1,000-4,999	5,000-19,999	20,000-99,000	100,000+	Total
25	44	21	8	2	100

Table 16   Tickets sold by type of festival

Type of festival	Average number of tickets sold at most recent festival
General arts	3,500
Mixed music	2,200
Classical	1,805
Jazz	1,500
Single art form	3,000
Folk	755
All festivals	2,000

19 festivals in our survey, 5% of the total, sold no tickets for festival events. These were not unsuccessful affairs but festivals in which all events were free – largely carnivals, jazz and waterfront festivals. Most festivals include free events in their programmes, but many were not able to provide us with accurate figures on the number of attendances at such events. Of the festivals that provided an estimated figure, 50% reported attendances of 1,500 or more. Five festivals reported attendances at free events of over 100,000 (see Table 17).

Table 17   Festivals with more than 100,000 attendances at free events

Festival	Attendances at free events
Edinburgh Festival Fringe	140,000
Cardiff Summer Festival	150,000
Dickens Festival in Rochester	250,000
Edinburgh International Festival	500,000
Notting Hill Carnival	1,500,000

Chapter 1 referred to the growth of new arts festivals in the 1980s. We reported some concern among festival organisers that the number is reaching saturation point and that festivals are competing for limited resources and could suffer as a result. To obtain data on this issue, and on perceptions of organisers about their festival's rate of growth, respondents to our postal survey were asked to compare the number of tickets sold and the numbers attending the 1991 festival with their 1986 festival. Both measures of growth were included in order to take account of the success of free events at arts festivals. The majority of festivals reported an increase in the number of people attending their festival over the five-year period and only 6% reported a decline in attendances. The number of festivals reporting a higher number of ticket sales was smaller than the number reporting increased attendances: 48% reported increased ticket sales but, again, the proportion reporting a decline was small, at 6%. Folk, single art form and classical music festivals were more likely than others to report a decline in ticket sales and attendances.

The festival audience

Few festivals can know the composition of their audience with any degree of accuracy. 35% of arts festivals have carried out a survey of audiences and attendances between 1986 and 1991 but, as we have already suggested, the detail of these surveys is variable. However, it is likely that most festivals have a reasonably accurate idea of the basic features of their audiences: the distance from which they travel, their age, social class and ethnic group. The majority of festivals in our survey (66%) reported having a largely local audience and 26% believed their audience to be largely from outside the area. General arts festivals are more likely to have a largely local audience, while jazz and folk festivals are more likely than others to have an audience from outside the area. The majority of festivals design the content of their programmes with the aim of attracting tourists in mind. Jazz and folk festivals were slightly more oriented towards attracting tourists than other festivals and single art form festivals less likely than others to have this consideration in mind.

Festivals undoubtedly play a role in attracting tourists to an area, and in generating income from tourism, although even the long-established arts festivals draw a substantial proportion of their audience from the local area. The impact on tourism is also likely to be far wider than attracting visitors simply for the duration of the festival, and we have already referred to the role of the arts in inner city regeneration.

Festival organisers clearly have an audience in mind when their programmes are developed and, in many cases, these will be people with an interest in the particular art form(s) featured in the festival. Organisers were asked if the programme was designed with particular sections of the population in mind, and 36% stated that they did aim to attract particular social groups. The sections of the population most frequently mentioned were those in particular age groups, especially young people, families and students.

Some festivals aim to attract middle-class people, presumably because they are considered to be more interested in the arts than working-class people. Our interview data suggest that festival audiences are disproportionately middle-class and that this applies particularly to the older, established arts festivals which are based on classical music. The audiences of these festivals are also predominantly middle-aged. They are not alone in this: folk festivals also report a high proportion of middle-class people and many festivals that take place outside the main centres of population tend to attract middle-aged or retired people. Some have attempted to broaden their appeal through programming and by staging a high proportion of free and out-of-doors events. For example, the Bristol Proms Festival attracts 50% of its audience from social classes C2, D and E and gives a higher number of concessions for pensioners and children than at other times of the year. One of its aims is to increase attendance at the Colston Hall at other times of the year, and this aim of increasing access to the arts is shared by many other festivals. Some festivals, for example the Camden Jazz Festival and the Aldeburgh Festival, approach this from the opposite angle, by staging events throughout the year some of which will attract people to the festival.

In addition to widening access to the arts, festivals also have a role in increasing the availability of less popular or well-known art forms, or individual works, to which even regular attenders at arts events have limited access. The Essex Festival aims to introduce the public to literature and poetry to which it would not otherwise have access, and likes to combine popular performances, which attract an audience, with less popular or well-known ones. For example, the festival included performances by two less well-known poets in a performance by a well-known boogie-woogie pianist.

The reasons why people attend arts festivals are diverse and, in some cases, the programme may be only one factor among many. As our survey shows, folk festivals are often held over a weekend and are often staged as an 'all-in-one' event which includes the price of a camp-site place in the ticket. These festivals tend to attract a high proportion of family groups and a following of regular attenders. Other festivals also report a loyal following among their audience, some of whom are members of a festival 'friends' organisation.

Many festivals are seeking to change the social composition of their audience. Some are attempting to attract young people through the festival content, or by changing the festival's image. For example, in order to attract a higher number of young people, the Sidmouth Festival of International Folk Arts is lowering the profile of ritual dancing, which attracts an older, more traditional, folk audience, and increasing the number of roots and world music events. It is also increasing the number of children's events and has found that adults are attracted to the festival because of the entertainment provided for their children. A number of other festivals in our survey planned to increase the number of children's events to attract a younger audience and more families (see Chapter 2). Other festivals, including the Aldeburgh Festival, have concentrated on changing the festival's image, which has included redesigning publications in order to attract a younger public as well as regular supporters of the festival. The Aldeburgh Festival has also aimed to attract young people to rehearsals and has formed a 'young friends' organisation. A limiting factor in its ability to attract a greater number of young people is the age profile of the local population. Other festivals also feel constrained by local demographic factors, or at least regard the scope for audience expansion as lying outside the local area. The key group is often seen as people within relatively easy travelling distance and who do not require over-night accommodation, which can be costly and in short supply during the festival season. The Edinburgh International Festival is particularly constrained in this respect and aims to increase its Scottish audience living outside the city.

Some festivals have been enterprising in their efforts to attract new audiences. For example, the Llanelli Festival has approached residential homes for the elderly to organise block bookings, and the Sidmouth International Festival of Folk Arts is targeting coach operators within a two-hour drive of the town with a view to organising a package that will include a coach trip, a cream tea and a festival performance within a fixed price. Some festivals are limited in the extent to which they can target an outside audience by the proximity of other festivals and by political considerations which require some local authority-run festivals to give priority to the local electorate.

Some organisers want to increase the numbers of working-class festival-goers and people from ethnic minority groups. Here there is a choice of strategy: festivals have targeted groups either through publicity and community or schools work, or by attention to the festival programme. The latter has included staging art forms with a wide popular appeal, such as jazz and film. Some festivals see a danger in such developments, fearing that the festival could 'become all things to all men' (sic) and lose its individual identity. However, if festivals target specific groups with particular cultural or artistic interests the festival's identity can be sharpened rather than blurred. For example, the London Film Festival aims to increase its ethnic minority audience by showing films with a 'Third World' theme and sending publicity material to relevant organisations and groups. The Camden Jazz Festival aims to attract people from ethnic minority groups, women and people with disabilities both through its publicity and through its programming by featuring artists from these social groups. The risk of this strategy is in achieving well-targeted but small audiences which can place a strain on festival finances. However, it can also result in higher attendances at 'mainstream' events from new audiences.

One festival organiser expressed the view that encouraging working-class festival-goers would necessitate lowering the festival's standards, which he was not prepared to countenance. This view was not widely held among the festival organisers. Many identified the principal barrier to achieving a more heterogeneous audience in the reluctance of many people to cross the threshold of arts venues. Theatres and concert halls are viewed by many people as places only for the wealthy and the artistically initiated. Many festival organisers believe that if attitudes to the venues can be changed, much of the battle will be won and that the festival can play a role in enticing non-attenders to arts events once this is achieved. However, it is not just people's perceptions of arts venues that discourages them from attending arts events.

Some festival organisers believe that ticket prices play an important role in discouraging less well-off people from attending arts performances and that low ticket prices during a festival season can encourage attendance at the festival and break down the barriers to enjoying the arts. Indeed, a number of festivals claim some success in this. Ticket prices are a central policy issue for organisers and, while most are concerned to keep ticket prices low, they are usually constrained by their own levels of funding and the cost of engaging performers and hiring venues. Many festivals offer price concessions to particular social groups, including pensioners, students and the unemployed, and offer a discount for bookings for a series of performances. These have been found to be successful in many cases.

Few festival organisers know the extent to which ticket prices influence audience figures in general, and they are not able to know with any degree of certainty what the relationship is between ticket prices and the class composition of festival-goers: 35% of organisers (excluding folk festivals) have conducted surveys of their audience, but while these can provide information on who attends the festival, they cannot tell why other people do not attend. One festival concluded that ticket prices did not deter people from attending, on the basis of responses to a questionnaire distributed to festival goers, a method with obvious limitations. The organisers of the Cricklade Festival, on the other hand, believe that 'a substantial slice of the population is deprived of quality live music' because of high ticket prices, and they have adopted a strategy of charging low prices in order to attract a wide section of the population. There is clearly a need for festivals to explore the potential for attracting new audiences or increasing the attendance of particular groups, and here they require research which goes beyond surveys of their existing audiences. Their ability to commission such research is clearly determined by their financial position. Meanwhile, the price elasticity of demand for arts performances and attendances should be better known (Millward Brown International, 1991).

Finally, it has to be said that some festivals are highly resistant to change in their audience. A concern to retain the original identity of a festival, fashioned by its founders many decades ago, was reported in a number of cases to be held most strongly by a festival committee which had actively opposed the organisers' proposals for change. However, the majority view is that festivals should attract as wide a span of the population as possible and should aim to attract new audiences, including young people and people from ethnic minority groups. The heterogeneity of festival audiences is not the sole factor behind funding decisions: festivals serve other purposes, of encouraging innovation and supporting new artists. However, it is felt that the case for public funding is considerably strengthened if the festival audience is not drawn exclusively from a privileged, or relatively privileged, minority of the population.

Media coverage

The media have a crucial role in publicising and promoting festival events. The extent of coverage and the nature of reviews can have a great influence on a festival's future well-being both in terms of its popularity among the general public and the attitude of funding bodies, including business sponsors. Most of the festival organisers interviewed reported good relations with the local press, although in many cases this had been established as a result of much effort on the part of festival staff and through contacts with sympathetic individuals. One organiser stated that it had been necessary for the staff to 'move mountains' to develop good relations with the local press, and that they had still been largely unsuccessful in getting much serious coverage. Personal contact with local journalists was considered essential because press releases are not usually followed up. Festivals also reported that the local press frequently printed previews but rarely reviewed actual festival performances.

Work with schools was found to attract positive media coverage, and there is scope for festivals to co-operate with the local press in this area of activity. For example, the Essex Festival organised a poetry competition in partnership with a local paper. The paper advertised the competition, the festival organiser judged the entries and the prize was presented at the festival by novelist Fay Weldon. A number of other festival organisers have attracted media coverage by staging newsworthy or televisual events. For example, the 1991 Bradford Festival was launched with the arrival of a Martian from a spaceship in the town centre.

Organisers complain of the difficulty in achieving serious coverage of festival events and a tendency on the part of the local press, in particular, to seek out trivia and scandal. The organisers of the Sidmouth Festival of International Folk Arts were dismayed when a story about an argument between a Norwegian coach driver and a traffic warden reached the front page of a local paper, while the arguably more impressive performance of the Norwegian choir went unreported.

Folk festival organisers believe that they suffer from a stereotypical image of folk enthusiasts as men in arran sweaters with beards and beerguts, which is at worst perpetuated and at best unchallenged by the media's treatment of folk festivals. They feel that the general public is left unaware of the range of art forms and styles covered by folk festivals. In general, however, festivals find that the limited media coverage which they are given is positive.

Some festival organisers therefore complained that the artistic content of their festival went unreported in favour of other aspects, while others found it regrettable that the coverage of arts events was restricted to the arts and entertainments pages. Clearly, festivals have mixed experiences in this regard and the principal request is for serious coverage that reflects the variety of the entertainment, the standard of performances and the experience of the audience. A number of festivals felt that they would like to make efforts to improve relations with both local and national press, but that their resources were insufficient to do so.

Radio and television coverage

39% of festivals (excluding folk) had festival performances or events broadcast on radio or television. General arts festivals and jazz festivals were more likely than others to have broadcasts, and festivals whose performances were broadcast were, on average, larger in terms of number of performances than those which did not receive such treatment. Most broadcasts of festival performances or events were radio rather than television broadcasts. Almost a third of all festivals had performances or events broadcast on radio and 55% of these had one or two broadcasts. Only 10 festivals reported having more than 10 broadcasts at their most recent festival: these included the Cheltenham Music Festival (11 radio broadcasts), the Aldeburgh Festival and the Edinburgh Book Festival (12 broadcasts), the Bath International Festival (13 radio broadcasts), the Belfast Festival at Queens (20 radio broadcasts) and the BBC Henry Wood Promenade Concerts (67 broadcasts).

Just under 16% of festivals had performances or events from their most recent festival broadcast on television and, again, the majority (57%) of these had one or two broadcasts. 7 festivals had more than 10 broadcasts: these included the BBC Henry Wood Promenade Concerts (12 broadcasts), the Cardiff Summer Festival and the

Edinburgh International Festival (15 broadcasts), and the Royal National Eisteddfod of Wales with broadcasts amounting to a total of 30 hours television coverage. In the case of the larger festivals, broadcasts are likely to have been on national radio or television, rather than on local stations, but we do not know whether this is true of festival radio broadcasting in general.

Festival organisers were asked about their experiences of radio and television coverage. Experiences of local radio were mixed, but it was generally felt that, while local stations are often good at publicising events, they rarely give serious coverage. Experiences of regional television were also found to be varied, but a particular problem was identified in the reluctance of regional television journalists to cover weekend events and events outside regional centres.

With regard to national coverage, festival organisers frequently stated that, while the national press produced lists of previews, and therefore served a useful role in advertising festival events, it rarely reviewed festival performances. They expressed frustration at the apparent reluctance of the press to leave London to attend any festival other than the larger, more prestigious ones, which receive international as well as national press coverage. They feel that serious reviews of performances would assist their applications for funding and business sponsorship, as well as increasing ticket sales and encouraging new audiences. National media coverage is also of benefit to individual artists, who include press clippings in their portfolios.

Experiences of national radio and television were similar: that the 'glossy' festivals attracted much media attention while most others were ignored. A number of festivals felt that a festival is a 'gift' for television since it offers a range of events, often featuring major artists. They therefore identified television coverage as a key untapped area of publicity, of which new independent stations might take advantage.

Key points

- In 1991 arts festivals sold an estimated total of 4.2 million tickets, ranging from 90 to over half a million with a median of 2,000. General arts festivals and festivals covering single art forms have higher than average ticket sales.

- About half of all festivals reported a higher number of ticket sales and attendances compared with their 1986 festival and only a small proportion reported a decline.

- Festivals have a higher concentration in areas of the country which attract tourists, and the majority of festival organisers design the programme content with the attraction of tourists in mind. Jazz and folk festivals are slightly more oriented towards attracting tourists than other festivals.

- Many festival organisers are seeking to change their audience in some way, by increasing attendances from young people, or from people outside the local area.

- Strategies developed to change the audience profile include targeting particular groups through publicity and community or schools work or by alterations to the festival programme which have included staging performances with a wide popular appeal and art forms such as jazz and film.

- 39% of festivals (excluding folk) had festival performances from their most recent festival broadcast on radio or television. General arts and jazz festivals were more likely to be broadcast than other types and most broadcasts were on radio rather than television. Less than 16% of festivals had performances or events from their most recent festival broadcast on television.

- Although some of the most prestigious arts festivals succeed in attracting very considerable media coverage, many festival organisers expressed dismay at the limited extent of coverage given by the media to arts festivals outside London, and to reviews of festival performances.

4 Festival Staffing

Introduction

One of the more tangible benefits of festivals is their impact on employment. Festivals generate temporary employment, for many thousands of professional artists. They also create permanent and temporary employment for many thousands of other people in their planning, organisation and operation. The majority (62%) of festivals employ paid staff, but a smaller proportion (38%) employ full-time staff than the proportion employing part-time staff (53%). Folk festivals are less likely to employ either full-time or part-time staff than other festivals (see Table 18).

Table 18   Staffing of arts festivals

Percentages

Type of festival	Employing paid staff	Not employing paid staff	Total	Number
General arts	72	28	100	138
Mixed music	62	38	100	29
Classical	61	39	100	36
Jazz	61	39	100	31
Folk	27	73	100	70
Single art form	87	13	100	45
Total	62	38	100	349

The number of staff employed by festivals is shown in Table 19. General arts, single art form and jazz festivals are over-represented among festivals with higher than average numbers of employees, and mixed music and folk festivals are over-represented among those with lower than average numbers of employees.

Table 19 **Number of paid staff employed by arts festivals**

Percentages

1	2-3	4-5	6-10	11-20	21+	No paid staff	Total
10	18	9	10	7	6	38	100

Festivals are therefore small employers and only a small proportion employ more than 20 full-time or more than 30 part-time staff. These are predominantly festivals run by local authorities or arts centres where staff are employed on other duties. They also tend to be festivals which employ a high proportion of their staff on a temporary basis, often for the festival period only.

Arts festivals (excluding folk festivals) in the survey were asked to give the percentage of their staff employed on a permanent or a temporary basis. Only 18% reported employing all of their staff on a permanent basis and in only 29% were the majority of staff permanent. Those employing all of their employees on permanent contracts are, in general, festivals run by a very small number of paid staff assisted by a team of volunteers for the festival period. Two exceptions to this are the Hay on Wye Festival of Literature which employs all its 3 full-time and 6 part-time staff on a permanent basis, and the Royal National Eisteddfod of Wales which employs 21 staff, mostly full-time, all the year round.

The reasons for reliance on temporary staff include the cyclical nature of much of the work involved, and the limitations and uncertainty surrounding the funding of many festivals. These are also factors behind the employment of staff on self-employed contracts. 36% of festivals hire staff on this basis, and 20% of all arts festivals (excluding folk) employ at least half of their staff on such contracts. The festivals in which all staff are self-employed cover a range of types but classical music festivals are more likely than others to be organised by a self-employed workforce.

Festival organisers (excluding folk) were also asked whether any staff were seconded from business to the festival and if the festival provided placements for people on government training schemes. Only a minority reported staffing their festivals from either of these sources: 3% had staff seconded from business and 10% provided placements to people on government training schemes.

Staff carry out a wide range of duties, including artistic direction and programming, publicity, general administration, sales, secretarial work, catering, cleaning, stewarding and fund-raising. In over half of all festivals paid staff are employed to carry out administration, publicity and secretarial tasks. The majority also use volunteers for administration and publicity work. Most festivals do not use paid staff for other duties. More use volunteers than paid staff for sales work, stewarding and fund-raising. Catering is usually carried out by outside contractors or volunteers. Almost equal proportions use volunteers, outside contractors or paid staff for cleaning duties. This does not exhaust the long list of tasks associated with organising and running a festival. As an organiser of the Wolds Festival, a community arts festival, reported:

> The two paid workers and six other committee members did *everything* – arranged flowers, organised food, swept floors, ferried equipment about, took down bunting, stuck up posters, delivered tickets, changed window displays (and) counted the money.

The cyclical nature of festival activities requires many to hire additional staff on an indirect basis through the contracting out of services. The majority (52%) of arts festivals (excluding folk) used outside contractors at their most recent festival. They were most usually hired for catering (38%) and cleaning (23%) Other activities contracted out by more than 10% of festivals are publicity, sales and stewarding. Festivals also reported contracting out sound and lighting, site and stage construction and security.

Staff and volunteers

Staffing issues are a central concern of festival organisers. Five of the 16 organisers interviewed spontaneously identified staffing as an area of priority if additional funding were to become available. Three of these currently employ staff who are over-stretched outside the festival period as well as during the festival. Another organiser, who did not refer directly to staffing as a priority area, reported high levels of turnover among staff for whom the volume of work and the pressure to create a successful event were intolerable. The other organisers who raised the issue of finance for staffing were from festivals which are run voluntarily, and one organiser estimated that if the organisers were paid, the festival would cost four times as much to run. This organiser also commented on the difficulties of volunteer-run festivals in achieving the professional approach expected by funding bodies and sponsors.

This is not to say that many volunteer-run festivals are not highly successful, expertly run events, but that this is achieved, in many cases, through efforts which are rewarded only in non-financial terms. Our current research confirms the earlier findings (Hutchison and Feist, 1991; Myerscough et al., 1988) that a large number of festivals rely heavily on voluntary help. Indeed, 38% are run entirely by volunteers. Many festival organisers work in full-time jobs and find that the festival takes much of their spare time. It is also apparent that many women and retired people without full-time paid employment devote substantial amounts of time and effort to arts festivals and that many individuals and households therefore provide an indirect subsidy in this area.

Organisers were asked to give the number of volunteers involved in the organisation of their festival, for the period of the festival only, and for the festival period and throughout the year. The number of volunteers for the period of the festival only ranged from 0 to 1,000, with half of all festivals using 10 or fewer volunteers. Only 19 festivals reported using more than 100 volunteers for the festival period and over half of these were arts festivals. The range in the number of volunteers for the festival and throughout the year was narrower at between 0 and 300, with half of all festivals using 5 or fewer volunteers. Only 9 festivals reported using the services of more than 50 volunteers during the year.

The 3 festivals with the highest number of volunteers for the festival period are the Sidmouth International Festival of Folk Arts (500 volunteers), the Llangollen International Musical Eisteddfod (900 volunteers) and the Royal National Eisteddfod of Wales (1,000 volunteers). The 3 festivals reporting the highest numbers for the festival period and throughout the year are the Aldeburgh Festival (70 volunteers), the Cleveland International Eisteddfod (90 volunteers) and, again, the Royal National Eisteddfod of Wales (300 volunteers).

The majority of festivals (excluding folk) use volunteers for administration, publicity and stewarding. However, of these, only stewarding is mainly a voluntary activity; the majority of festivals also use paid staff for administration and publicity. A higher proportion use volunteers for stewarding, sales, catering and fund-raising than use paid staff for these duties. 74% of festivals use voluntary stewards and 48% use volunteers for fund-raising.

Many festivals have a friends' association, established to raise funds and sometimes to assist with festival organisation. In 21% of all festivals volunteers are from a friends' association. The Royal National Eisteddfod of Wales and the Glyndebourne Festival Opera were the festivals with the largest income from this source, although the latter does not involve volunteers in running the festival.

Limitations on the use of volunteers

24% of festivals make no use of volunteers, the principal reason being the need for staff to work intensively in terms of hours and effort, which it was felt could not be expected of voluntary help. For many volunteers, commitment to the festival and the pleasure at being able to participate and contribute to its success are reward enough; many volunteers are arts enthusiasts, and this applies particularly to folk festivals where amateur performers frequently perform stewarding duties. However, some festival organisers are concerned that the festival should offer volunteers something in return for their efforts in terms of training or other benefit. Festivals often find difficulty in providing these rewards and therefore choose not to use volunteers. A concern was also expressed by organisers that volunteers sometimes expect to receive the offer of a future paid job, which is simply an unrealistic expectation. A further limitation lies in potential security problems when volunteers are used for box office or duties which involve handling cash. Perhaps the most labour-intensive organisational work of the Edinburgh Festival is the handling of cash and box office work and for this reason it prefers to employ paid staff. Some festivals prefer to hire students on minimal rates of pay, with varying degrees of formality from cash in hand for stewarding festival performances to offering placements on relevant college courses.

The principal problem with reliance on voluntary help in festival duties was found to lie in the limited control that organisers have over volunteers. As one organiser put it, 'They won't do as they're told and you have no control over them'. A volunteer is under no contractual obligation to be present at particular times or to perform particular duties. In addition, conflict sometimes occurs when volunteers are critical of what they see as 'commercialisation' or excessive professional input. A power struggle can therefore result with damaging consequences. For example, one organiser of a prestigious music festival expressed the view that some volunteers are motivated by the social cachet to be had from being associated with the festival. This festival had found it necessary to carry out two big 'clear-outs' of voluntary stewards within ten years because 'they thought they were more important than the festival'.

Festival staff often take great care in the selection of volunteers, so that motives and abilities can be subjected to some degree of scrutiny. The quality of volunteers is particularly important when they are used for stewarding duties because, as one festival organiser put it, 'To the general public, the stewards are the festival directors'. In some cases they are selected by a friends association, which was generally found to be an easier arrangement for the festival, although occasional conflicts still occurred. This formalises the division between professional organisation and voluntary support and appears to serve the purpose of reducing conflict between what are often two different orientations to the festival.

Many festivals have found that conflict has arisen when volunteers have worked alongside paid staff, sometimes because volunteers have been treated as if they were paid, and 'team spirit' can be compromised in these circumstances. It was also suggested that continuity and accumulation of experience are problematic if there is heavy reliance on volunteers, but this appears to be a minority view since many festivals report a loyal and long-serving band of helpers. One way to avoid the bad feeling that can arise between festival staff who sometimes feel that their volunteers lack discipline and volunteers who make unfavourable comparisons between their unpaid efforts and those of paid staff, is to assign entirely separate duties to the two groups. PSI's report on the amateur arts (Hutchison and Feist, 1991) refers to the problems that can arise in the use of volunteers in conjunction with paid staff, and a report by the Office of Arts and Libraries suggests that the tasks of paid staff and volunteers should be clearly delineated. Some festivals appear to adopt this practice. For example, the Edinburgh Festival uses volunteers to do the mailings and work on the information desk, and the Bradford Festival involves volunteers in the community events. Some festivals have also found that organising volunteers under separate supervision has helped to prevent problems of co-ordination and conflict with paid staff. This is a similar solution to having a separate friends' organisation perform the task.

Training and management needs of arts festivals

Hutchison and Feist's 1991 report on the amateur arts concludes, on the question of volunteers, that 'for volunteering to be successful, it requires effective aims and objectives, management and training'. The 16 festival organisers interviewed in our survey were asked about their general training and management needs. Arts festivals have become more aware of the importance of training, not only as a result of the prominence of training issues on the national political agenda, but also because of an awareness of the economic, as well as cultural, importance of the arts.

The major part of the training of festival staff is done in post, but festivals are increasingly making use of, or considering the benefits of, off-the-job training on specialist courses. The most frequently mentioned training need was in marketing, because lack of expertise in this area was thought to be resulting in lost opportunities, particularly in attracting new audiences. Fund-raising, and particularly obtaining sponsorship, was also an area where festivals felt the need for training and assistance. Some festivals, including ones that are volunteer-run, had access to such courses through their regional arts boards, and thought it essential that courses should be designed to meet the needs of arts organisations. A number of organisers expressed the view that arts organisations are currently poorly catered for and require specialist advice. One organiser described arts festivals as half-way between national charities and sports organisations: they are not as deserving as charities and do not have the mass appeal of sports organisations.

A second area where festival organisers thought training would be beneficial is in management skills. We referred above to the use of volunteers and the need to adopt different approaches to voluntary and paid staff. We also referred to the intensity of work during the festival period, which can result in anxiety and tension between festival staff. Nervous or anxious performers may also need to be handled with care, and a number of organisers referred to difficulties in dealing with the numerous demands made on staff during the festival period. Here again, the need for specialised courses was raised, particularly because it was felt that many arts festivals cannot be as 'hard-nosed' as standard businesses, since they rely on voluntary help and the goodwill of many participants.

One area in which skill requirements are similar to those of a wide range of other organisations is in computing. Many festivals have introduced computer systems for a whole range of functions, including bookings, mailing lists and finances. Some organisers had used outside training courses, but, in some cases, formal training was minimal or was given to one member of staff who then passed on the knowledge to others.

A few organisers also identified a need for training in general administration. This was particularly felt by the folk festivals, which have less of a tradition of professional involvement on the organisational side as well as in performances, and therefore often suffer from a shortage of expertise in basic administration.

Ideally, festivals can identify their training needs and arrange for them to be met by appointing a development officer, and this was the approach adopted by the Edinburgh Fringe Festival. However, other festivals, particularly those that are volunteer-run, are not able to fund such a post. As one organiser remarked, the festivals and festival staff who are most in need of training are too busy to attend training courses. Another organiser commented that, before a festival could consider training issues, it would need to increase its number of staff. Because the benefits of training are not evident in the short term, training tends to be viewed as a low priority for festival funds. Interview data suggest that this is as true of large comparatively well-off festivals as of smaller ones.

Finally, although our research suggests that festivals' needs for training and staff development are not being met in all cases, there may also be benefits to be gained by leaving some aspects of festival organisation to specialists, through sub-contracting. We referred above to the extent of contracting-out in such matters as cleaning and catering, but festivals can also adopt this practice for areas in which they lack expertise rather than manpower. For example, the Bury St Edmunds Festival contracts out the job of selling advertising space in its programme. Clearly, it can be costly to use specialist contract staff, and their use may be limited for this reason. However, the organisation of a festival involves a range of highly skilled activities, which it may well have difficulty in developing in-house.

Key points

- The majority (62%) of festivals employ paid staff to organise and run the festival programme. The majority of folk festivals are run entirely by volunteers.

- Festivals employ paid staff principally for artistic direction, programming, administration, publicity and secretarial tasks.

- 76% of festivals have help from volunteers either during the year or for the period of the festival. Volunteers are used principally for sales work, stewarding and fund-raising.

- The majority of festival staff are employed on a temporary basis because of the cyclical nature of much of the work involved and the limitations and uncertainty surrounding the funding of many festivals. Many festival staff are employed on self-employed contracts. 20% of all festivals (excluding folk) employ at least half of their staff on this basis and the need for flexibility in staffing arrangements may be an influential factor.

- The majority of festivals contracted out services integral to their most recent festival. Catering and cleaning were the two services provided most frequently on this basis.

- Festival organisers feel the need for training in marketing, fund-raising – particularly in obtaining sponsorship – and in management skills.

5 Funding

Introduction

The total annual income of arts festivals in the UK is estimated to be £40.6 million. The principal sources of income are box office receipts, which amounted to an estimated total of £17.6 million in 1991, business sponsorship, from which festivals received an estimated income of £6.8 million, and funding from local authorities and local arts councils, which amounted to an estimated total of £7 million. These sources account for 41, 13 and 11% of festival income respectively. Table 20 shows the variation by type of festival in main sources of income. Festival income ranges from £115 to over £5.5

Table 20   Main sources of income by festival type

Percentages

	General arts	Mixed music	Classical music	Jazz	Single art form	Folk
Box office	37	37	44	47	26	51
Business sponsorship	18	16	15	15	7	3
Local authority/ local arts association	16	11	3	12	10	11
All public sources (local authority/ local arts association, regional arts board, national arts councils	25	17	12	17	20	14
Other*	20	30	29	21	48	34
Total	100	100	100	100	100	100

*   includes friends' associations, donations and other earned income (e.g. from catering, sales of goods or programmes)

Table 21   Range in total income of arts festivals

						Percentages
£100-9,999	£10,000-29,000	£30,000-49,000	£50,000-99,999	£100,000-499,000	£500,000+	Total
31	28	8	12	17	4	100

million, with a median of £22,000. 30% of festivals have an income of less than £10,000. See Table 21 for the distribution of festivals by income.

The total annual expenditure of festivals is estimated to be £40.9 million, the largest items being professional artists' fees, publicity and marketing, hire of venues and equipment and administration. Festival expenditure ranges from £375 to over £5.5 million with a median of £23,000. The two festivals with the highest box office income are the Edinburgh International Festival and Glyndebourne Festival Opera, both of which took several £millions each at their most recent festivals. These two festivals alone account for over a third of all festival box office receipts and just 5 festivals take over 50% of all receipts. Glyndebourne (£5.5 million) and the Edinburgh International Festival (£4 million) also had the highest expenditure of all festivals.

Festivals attract a considerable amount of funding from a variety of sources, but they are expensive events to stage, and over half (51%)

Table 22   Festivals with an accumulated deficit, by type of festival

			Percentages
Type of festival	With an accumulated deficit	Without an accumulated deficit	Total
General arts	13	87	100
Mixed music	13	87	100
Classical	10	90	100
Jazz	20	80	100
Folk	12	88	100
Single art form	15	85	100
Total	13	87	100

reported that their most recent festival had incurred a deficit. It is for this reason that the average figure for total expenditure is higher than the figure for average income. A minority of festivals (13%) reported an accumulated deficit, and jazz festivals are more likely than other types to be in this position (see Table 22). But this still suggests that a substantial number of festivals are in financial difficulty.

Support from arts funding bodies

45% of festivals received income from their regional arts board for their most recent festival, with the amount of support ranging from £100 to £58,500. The estimated total income of festivals from this source in 1991 was £2 million and the median figure for funding received from this source was £1,150. Only 18% of festivals received more than £2,000. The festivals receiving the highest funding from this source, at over £30,000, were the Huddersfield Contemporary Music Festival (£31,000), the Bristol Proms Festival (55,000) and the London International Festival of Theatre (58,500). 20% received funding from National Arts Council for their most recent festival, with the amount of financial support ranging from £33 to £590,000. 10% of festivals received over £5,000 and 3 festivals received over £200,000: the Belfast Festival at Queen's University (£222,000), the London International Festival of Theatre (£255,000) and the Edinburgh International Festival (£590,000).

Over half of the festivals where we carried out interviews received funding from arts funding bodies, although in many cases the amounts involved were quite small. Experiences of regional arts boards varied widely: one organiser described the support that the festival receives from its regional arts board, Eastern Arts, as 'splendid – they support the festival up to the hilt', while another, in a different region, described the experience of dealing with his regional arts board as 'like banging your head against a brick wall'. There were several complaints that festivals are considered a low priority for funding, particularly in comparison with funding of concert halls and other arts venues. There was also a feeling that a regional arts board could not be expected to give substantial funding to one festival in its area because to do so would be unfair to other festivals. However, some organisers believe that favouritism exists with regard to the more prestigious arts festivals. Folk festival organisers are most vociferous on this issue and have campaigned for folk arts to be recognised as worthy of funding. This view appears to be gaining acceptance and is perhaps the result of growing professionalism and a more catholic approach to music of all kinds: for example, a bluegrass and roots festival in our survey reported an excellent relationship with its regional arts board.

Festival organisers reported an interest in funding innovative work among arts boards, although one organiser had found the arts board rather too directional in this respect. It was considered essential that arts boards encourage and fund innovative work or at least provide sufficient core funding for such work to be subsidised by popular events. A number of organisers reported generally low levels of public funding as limiting the innovatory content. In the experience of the Harrogate International Festival: 'Neither sponsors nor, unfortunately, audiences have shown commitment to support in necessary numbers contemporary or untried activities, forcing the festival... to increasingly limit programming new work'.

The support of national arts councils and regional arts boards was also considered necessary to pursue additional activities, including educational work and social needs projects where festivals can make a substantial contribution. For example, the Welsh Arts Council, among others, assists the Swansea Festival to fund a 'Live Music Now' programme that stages performances in hospitals, prisons, schools and residential homes where people are unable, for whatever reason, to attend the festival. Again, financial support is essential because activities of this type cannot be self-supporting.

Festival organisers feel, perhaps unfairly, that funding decisions are sometimes based on the personal tastes of arts board staff, which can work in a festival's favour or to its disadvantage. A number of organisers remarked on what they saw as an absence of clear guidelines on funding decisions, which gave scope to the prejudices and preferences of individual officers. As one organiser of a community arts festival in our survey remarked: 'Regional arts bodies appear to have no cohesive policies. The parameters for funding change from year to year and from region to region and appear to have more to do with personalities and interests of staff rather than any national or even regional policy.' A number of organisers identified an additional problem in the timing of decisions, which is often found to be late; funding may not be confirmed until an artist or group has been booked. The inconvenience and expense involved can be particularly frustrating if a refusal is given on the basis of a policy of which festival organisers were not previously aware.

Local authority support for arts festivals

17% of festivals are directly run by a local authority and these receive substantial financial support and support in kind from this source. However, 75% of all festivals receive some funding from local authorities or local arts councils. The total income to festivals from this source in 1991 is estimated at £7 million. These funds account for an average of 11% of total festival income. The amount received ranges from £75 to over £80,000 with a median of £1,500.

General arts festivals are more likely than others to receive funding from these sources, and, in particular, are more likely to receive substantial financial support. Over half of all festivals receiving in excess of £5,000 from a local authority or local arts association for their most recent festival were general arts festivals. Folk festivals were the least likely to receive substantial funding from these sources.

The three festivals in our survey with the highest income from local authorities are the Royal National Eisteddfod of Wales (£187,000), the Brighton International Festival (£250,000)and the Edinburgh International Festival (£80,000), none of which are run by a local authority.

53% of festivals received support in kind from local authorities for their most recent festival, 34% in the use of premises for performances, 31% in the use of premises for organisation and administration, 29% in the use of equipment, 26% in assistance with publicity and 21% through staff seconded to the festival.

Experiences of local authority support

Six of the festivals whose organisers we interviewed were established by a local authority. These festival organisers reported the arrangement as generally beneficial to the festival. It conferred substantial support in kind, including use of premises and staff, as well as funding for artists' fees and other direct festival expenditure. Most festival organisers working for local authorities felt that the authority, and particularly the councillors, valued the festival and saw it as making an important contribution to the borough's livelihood. There were also reports of the use of festivals as a 'political football' between parties concerned with promoting the best use of poll-tax payers money or with equal access to the arts. Some festival organisers reported political opposition to the festival on the grounds that it caters for a privileged minority of the local population, a criticism behind some festivals' attempts, as noted earlier, to widen their appeal in terms of social class and age. Ironically, however, some organisers felt financially restricted in the extent to which they could develop their festival in this way.

The status of a festival as a luxury item of expenditure in a council's budget was found to be the cause of much uncertainty, not necessarily over a festival's continuing existence, but over its scale and the content of its programme. This, combined with lengthy bureaucratic procedures, makes planning problematic for some local authority-run festivals. Some local authorities guarantee a festival's budget several years in advance, an arrangement which is of considerable help both to local authority-run festivals and to those which are independently organised but supported by the local authority.

We referred in Chapter 1 to the availability of a concert hall or other suitable or attractive venue for performances and events as an impetus behind the development of some festivals. The use of free or subsidised venues is clearly of major assistance to arts festivals. As noted above, 34% receive support in kind in the use of local authority premises for performances. The 1980s saw the gradual introduction of legislation enabling, and then requiring, local authorities to put some of their services out to tender. At the time of our survey this legislation had not yet been applied to the management of local authority buildings, such as theatres and concert halls, but there have been indications that legislation might be extended to cover this area. This was seen as a potential threat to the survival of festivals, which could find their costs escalating if the full economic costs were to be charged by a private contractor. It was thought that some local authorities find the possibility of contracting out attractive because it would relieve them of the responsibility of making venues pay throughout the year, and would transfer to festival staff the responsibility of ensuring the financial viability of staging events in particular venues.

Festival organisers reported a related development in the sale, or proposed sale, of venues owned by local authorities, as a result of financial pressures on poll-capped authorities. The Harrogate Festival had not been able to sign contracts over hall use for its 1992 festival because halls were on the market for private purchase.

Another area where festivals receive financial and in-kind support is in the field of education. More than half of the festivals whose organisers we interviewed had received assistance from county councils for educational work, through direct funding and advice. This assistance was found to be invaluable because of the perceived importance of cultivating a new, young, audience. In a few cases festivals had regular contact with a county council arts development officer. Festival organisers expressed much satisfaction with the quality of advice and assistance they received in this area.

Business sponsorship of arts festivals

76% of all arts festivals receive income from business sponsorship. In 1991 festivals received an estimated total of £6.8 million from this source accounting for an average of 13% of all festival income. The amount of sponsorship received by festivals for their most recent event ranged from £17 to over £500,000, the median being £1,950. General arts festivals receive higher than average income from business sponsorship and folk festivals receive lower than average levels of income from this source. 26% of festivals received more than £10,000 for their most recent festival from this source. The largest earner in this respect was, perhaps predictably, the Edinburgh International Festival. Other festivals attracting business sponsorship in excess of £100,000 were the Chichester Festival, the Cheltenham International Festival of Music, the Film Festivals of London and Edinburgh, the Brighton International Festival, the Aldeburgh Festival, the Bath International Festival, the Royal National Eisteddfod of Wales and Glyndebourne Festival Opera.

Businesses also provide festivals with much in-kind support. Over half of all festivals receive non-financial support from business, slightly fewer than the number receiving in-kind support from a local authority. The type of support given varies greatly between festivals. Secondment of staff is unusual: only 3% of festivals receive this type of help from business. The most common forms of support are in publicity and equipment, (26% of festivals), use of business premises (12%) and use of premises for organisation and administration, (10%). Other support given by business includes prizes for competitions, and provision of free refreshments, consultancy and legal advice.

Experiences of business sponsorship

Almost all the festival organisers interviewed received support in the form of business sponsorship, although the amounts involved varied widely. The main source of business sponsorship was reported to be from large companies with a presence in the local area, including retail stores, garages and banks. In financial terms large companies appear to be the main source of sponsorship, but the majority of companies giving sponsorship are small, often local, companies including local newspapers, building societies and law firms. However, in many cases, smaller companies provide support in kind rather than in financial terms, for example by producing publicity material or the festival programme (see below).

Festival organisers identified two motives for companies sponsoring events: promotion and client hospitality. Businesses see festivals as an opportunity to promote products in a direct sense, but also to promote the company image through association with a prestigious event. One festival reported another purpose behind sponsorship: a large retail company with an outlet in Bradford sponsored Asian events at the 1991 Bradford Festival because it saw the Asian community as a source for the recruitment of staff as well as sales.

As an article in *The Economist* of 5 August 1989 states, sponsors 'want a well-defined, high quality event aimed at a specific audience'. In the experience of most festival organisers, client entertainment and hospitality is one of the principal reasons behind business sponsorship. Festival organisers therefore report particular interest among business sponsors in orchestral performances which are likely to attract a large audience and be considered festival highlights. However, sponsorship is by no means restricted to these events and opera, other music performances, dance, drama and film were all reported as attractive to sponsors. With regard to arts and music festivals, the events for which festival organisers reported difficulty in obtaining sponsorship included international drama, visual arts, literature and some contemporary arts. Business is concerned that the events which it sponsors are enjoyed by its clients and is not willing to take a risk in sponsoring an unknown or unusual work.

The organisers of the Notting Hill Carnival have experienced difficulty in obtaining sponsorship as a consequence of inaccurate and adverse media coverage. Other festival organisers are also concerned that a distorted image of their festival has discouraged potential sponsors. Folk festival organisers in particular felt that their 'beards and beerguts' reputation even deterred the brewing companies, because the image masks the reality: namely, a high proportion of middle-class festival-goers with spending power, and a growing proportion of young people attracted to roots and world music, increasingly a feature of folk festivals. One folk festival organiser had been told by potential sponsors that folk festivals were not suitable venues for the promotion of their products. It appears therefore that the folk festivals in receipt of business sponsorship are supported by local companies aware of the audience composition through local knowledge. It is also apparent that individual business managers, with an interest in a particular art form, can be influential in securing sponsorship or support in kind for a local festival. The experiences of these festivals suggest that there is scope for businesses to sponsor festivals in order to promote products to target audiences, rather than to view festivals principally as opportunities for entertaining clients. To encourage this attitude, companies require information on the composition, as well as the size, of festival audiences, and this varies greatly between festivals in both availability and quality.

Most of the festival organisers interviewed were satisfied with their relationship with business sponsors and did not feel that sponsors tried to influence the festival unduly. In some cases sponsors are presented with a list of festival performances and events from which they make a choice. In other cases, regular sponsors are approached to obtain their views on the kinds of performances and events that they would like to sponsor. Most festival organisers expressed the view that business sponsorship or the potential for increasing funding in this area did not influence the festival programme. The London Film Festival divides its programme into sections and potential sponsors choose a whole section rather than separate performances, and have no influence on the section's content. In the case of this festival, client entertainment is a major reason for sponsorship and the festival organisers advise sponsors of any potentially offensive content in the film. In such a circumstance, sponsors might choose not to offer tickets to clients but would not withdraw their sponsorship.

While business sponsorship is not, in general, likely to result in the inclusion or exclusion of a particular event or performance, it is clearly more difficult to judge its more subtle and indirect influence.

Festival programmes are generally decided before business sponsorship is seriously discussed and secured; but ideas of what is likely to attract sponsorship may come into play and, in particular, festival organisers may be concerned to include a certain proportion of safe and popular events. Moreover, many festivals reported receiving sponsorship from the same companies each year, so that their preferences may be known and incorporated into decisions about the programme. Clearly, the major concern for most business sponsors is that the events for which they provide funding are popular and, for festivals, this consideration is likely to be most influential.

One possible problem with a reliance on business sponsorship therefore is that festival programmes become unadventurous and 'safe'. Festival organisers are aware of this tendency, but do not see it as a consequence of business sponsorship *per se* but as a result of inadequate guaranteed public funding, which increases the reliance both on 'safe' events and on funding from private sources. Given the funding difficulties experienced by many festivals, the problem was found to be not the influence of business sponsors but the extent of business sponsorship that they could secure. Many festivals that depend on business sponsorship for survival, as well as others which are without sponsorship, felt they were locked into a vicious circle where inadequate funding restricted their ability to carry out marketing and to seek funding from business and other sponsors. One festival director had taken the decision to confine sponsorship to a small, loyal, group. The problem faced by his successor was that the contributions of business sponsors had not been increased and the festival organisers feared that a request for an increase would result in a withdrawal of the existing support.

Several festival organisers have carried out trawls of potential sponsors by contacting several hundred companies by letter. This method was found to be easy, and relatively cheap, but not very successful. Direct personal approaches to key companies with a strong local presence usually prove to be more fruitful, but the ability of festivals to identify these companies depends on the local area, as well as the nature of the festival. The Notting Hill Carnival has been innovative in its attempts to secure business sponsorship by visiting organisers and sponsors of similar events in the USA. The organisers of the Notting Hill Carnival and several other festival organisers have identified a particular need for advice and assistance in this area, since they believe the scope for sponsorship and the benefits to be gained by business are considerable. A report commissioned by the Scottish Tourist Board on the Edinburgh Festivals identifies the attraction of sponsorship as an area where festivals could benefit from some assistance (Scottish Tourist Board, 1992).

We have referred to the uncertainties surrounding the provision of public funding from regional arts boards and local authorities. Festival organisers expressed the view that business sponsorship is particularly 'fickle', a problem of which some festivals have become acutely aware since the onset of economic recession in 1990. In December 1991 plans for the launch of a literature festival in London were shelved because the organisers failed to raise the necessary sponsorship from business, and several festival organisers reported a reluctance among businesses that had previously sponsored the festival to continue their support. This was not always for financial reasons, but out of industrial and public relations considerations. A company with a strong presence in the local community cannot be seen to be funding events or spending on advertising at the same time as it is freezing recruitment or making redundancies. Festivals are equally unhappy at accepting sponsorship in these circumstances, since their audiences are drawn predominantly from the local community, a proportion of which works for the sponsoring companies.

Other sources of income

In addition to the principal sources of festival income: box office, arts council or regional arts board, local authority and business sponsorship, festivals receive funding from friends' associations and festival trusts. We referred in Chapter 4 to the role of friends' associations and to their contribution to the funding of festival activities. 27% of festivals received income from this source.

48% of festivals receive donations from other sources, and the median amount received in donations in 1991 was £50. In some cases festivals have made successful applications for funding from charitable trusts or received funding from tourist boards or development boards. The Musicians' Union has also provided funding for festivals. For example, the Potteries Folk Festival received a grant of £1,000 and the Cornwall Folk Festival at Wadebridge received £500 from this source. Another area of revenue generation is sales of goods, including programmes, books, T-shirts and posters. Following advice from a consultant the Bath Festival quadrupled its income from this source according to *The Economist*, 5 August 1989. Other sources of funding include bank interest and income from advertising.

Festival expenditure

As noted earlier, the main items of expenditure for arts festivals are professional artists' fees, publicity and marketing, venue and equipment hire and administration expenses.

Festivals spent a median of £8,600 on professional artists' fees for their most recent festival. Those which spent the most in this area were the Brighton International Festival (£805,000), Glyndebourne Festival Opera (£2.2 million) and the Edinburgh International Festival (£2.4 million).

Festivals spent a median of £2,140 on publicity and marketing for their most recent festival. This is an area in which they also receive support in kind: 26% of festivals receive assistance with publicity from the local authority and the same proportion receive support in this respect from business. Four festivals spent over £10,000 on publicity and marketing for their most recent festival: the London International Festival of Theatre (£103,000), the Brighton International Festival (£11,000), the Edinburgh International Festival (£400,000) and the Edinburgh Festival Fringe (£227,000).

Festivals spent an average of £1,700 on venue and equipment hire for their most recent festival. This is also an area in which they receive support in kind: 29% use equipment supplied by the local authority and 26% receive support of this kind from business. Two festivals spent in excess of £500,000 on venue and equipment hire at their 1991 festivals: the Edinburgh International Festival (£530,000), and the Royal National Eisteddfod of Wales (£769,000).

Festivals spent a median of £1,080 on administration (excluding staffing costs) for their most recent festival. The two which spent the most in this field were Glyndebourne Festival Opera (£723,000) and the Edinburgh International Festival (£781,000).

Other areas of expenditure include hospitality and royalties incurred by 20% of festivals. 3 festivals paid more than £5,000 in royalties for performances at their most recent festival.

Changes in sources of income

In the postal survey we asked festivals if there had been any changes in their sources of income over the previous five years. 35% gave a positive answer to this question and a higher proportion of mixed music festivals (48%) reported change in this respect. In 38% of these cases, an increased proportion of present income was reported as coming from business sponsorship. This was not necessarily the result of any increase in this sponsorship, although this was true in some cases, but because income from public sources had declined. A number of festivals also reported a fall in business sponsorship, as a result of the recession. These included the Billingham International Folklore Festival, the Wolds Festival and the Windsor Fringe Festival.

Limitations on funding and spending priorities

Most of the festival organisers interviewed expressed the view that the funding of their festival was inadequate. This is not in itself surprising since, presumably, most festival organisers would prefer to have an unlimited budget and freedom to plan events regardless of cost. However, a number of organisers reported having to reduce the scale of events and even the length of the festival for financial reasons. A number of festivals in our survey had recently folded or faced an uncertain future for the same reason. The extent of the problem cannot be quantified, although future research might use the PSI data set for this purpose.

Limitations on funding do not necessarily make a festival unviable, but they can restrict the programme and activities in particular ways. In Chapter 2 we referred to commissioning and the presentation of innovative work as among the traditional purposes of arts festivals. We also referred to the financial restrictions on festivals in this regard. A number of festival organisers interviewed stated that they would like to include, or expand on the proportion of, innovative work in the festival. In a similar vein, a number reported that they could not afford to take risks and stage unusual works which might make a loss at the box office. Uncertainty surrounding a festival's funding can be equally damaging, making planning difficult and directing the energies of festival organisers away from programme planning to funding concerns. One festival, run by a poll-capped local authority, found planning particularly problematic because delays in funding decisions made it difficult to confirm bookings with artists.

The festival organisers interviewed were asked what they would do with additional funding. A number see the extension of their festival, either in length or in scope, as a priority; several organisers want to include more non-music arts events. A second area was identified as staffing (see above and Chapter 4). One organiser of a voluntary-run festival felt that the festival could achieve higher standards of professionalism, particularly in its approach to funding bodies and sponsors, if funding was available to pay a full- or part-time organiser. Facilities for artists, the public and the press were identified as a further area in which festivals could benefit from additional funding. Particularly worrying were the concerns of one festival organiser that the festival was not fulfilling its obligations under the health and safety legislation because it could not afford to do so. A number of festivals identified expenditure on venues as a priority, either in terms of the need to hire larger and better venues or to repair or refurbish existing ones. This is discussed further in Chapter 6.

Other areas identified as priorities for additional funding are a higher proportion of international artists, a greater involvement in educational work and improved marketing.

Key points

- The total annual income of arts festivals in the UK is estimated to be £40.6 million.

- The principal sources of income are box office receipts, amounting to an estimated total of £17.6 million; business sponsorship, amounting to an estimated total of £6.8 million; and local authorities/local arts associations, amounting to an estimated £7 million.

- The total annual expenditure of arts festivals is estimated to be £40.9 million.

- The largest items of expenditure are professional artists' fees, publicity and marketing, hire of venues and equipment hire and administration.

- Over half of all festivals reported that their most recent festival incurred a deficit. 13% of festivals reported having an accumulated deficit.

- 45% of festivals received income from their regional arts board for their most recent festival and the total income from this source was estimated to be £2 million in 1991.

- 20% of festivals reported receiving funding from a national arts council for their most recent festival.

- Some festival organisers feel a need for clear guidelines on the funding criteria of the regional arts boards.

- Only 17% of festivals are directly run by a local authority but 75% receive some funding from a local authority or local arts council. The median amount received in 1991 was £1,500. General arts festivals are more likely than other festivals to receive funding from this source and folk festivals are least likely to receive any. Local authorities also provide much support in kind: 53% of arts festivals received funding from this source for their most recent festival, most usually in the use of premises and equipment and in assistance with publicity.

- Some festivals which are reliant on local authority support feel that their future is threatened by the uncertainty surrounding local authority funding. Some festivals have already been affected by the sale of local authority venues.

- Festivals receive an estimated total of £6.8 million in business sponsorship and the amount received by individual festivals ranges from £17 to over £500,000. The median amount of business sponsorship received by festivals in 1991 was £1,950 and business sponsorship accounted for a median of 13% of all festival income. General arts festivals receive higher than average sponsorship from business, and folk festivals report the lowest level of support from this source.

- Over half of all festivals receive support in kind from business.

- Festival organisers do not feel that sponsors exert a direct influence on the festival programme, but the subtle and indirect influence is more difficult to assess. Organisers are aware of the tendency towards 'safe' programming but do not see it as a consequence of business sponsorship per se, but of inadequate guaranteed public funding.

- 35% of festivals reported that their sources of income had recently changed, and in many cases increased reliance on business sponsorship was the key change.

- Festival organisers identified increasing the proportion of innovative work, extending the duration of the festival and raising staffing levels as priorities if festival income were to be increased.

6 The Future of Arts Festivals

Festivals' evaluation methods

Chapter 1 examined the purposes of arts festivals which arise from their context, their target audience and their general or specific aims and objectives. In the interview stage of our study festival organisers were asked about how they evaluated the success or otherwise of their festival. Methods used were found to vary widely, but in most circumstances took the form of monitoring rather than evaluation in a real sense. Festival organisers engage in evaluation principally when they become aware of problems in the existing direction and feel it necessary to review the festival programme, its marketing or some other aspect of the festival. This has prompted festivals to make various changes, including the promotion of educational work and the broadening out of music festivals to cover a range of forms (see Chapter 5). The methods of evaluation vary according to the constitution and, for professionally run festivals, evaluation can be an area of conflict between festival staff and committees or trusts. More formal systems of evaluation are likely to operate for festivals that are run by local authorities. Chapter 5 referred to the issues that arise in the evaluation of these festivals, including the accessibility of the festival to groups represented in the local population. Financial viability is, in most cases, an essential requirement for a festival's survival and is therefore closely monitored. However, in itself, it is not generally recognised as an appropriate measure of a festival's success, although it can indicate good budgeting, appropriate ticket pricing and well-judged attendances.

Although in the evaluation of most artistic events and performances both qualitative and quantitative factors need to be judged and weighed, the principal means by which festivals evaluate their success is through examining the size of audiences and attendances. As one festival organiser argued, capacity audiences are a sign that a festival is 'hitting the right note'. However, another organiser argued, equally legitimately, that he is not 'a promoter of popular concerts' and that in his view an event could be considered a success even if it attracted only 10 people; it was the quality of performances about which he expressed a particular concern.

Festival organisers seek the views of their audience by various means. 35% of festivals have carried out a survey of their audience and some festival organisers report this as being very useful in obtaining feedback. The Edinburgh Fringe Festival provides an incentive to festival goers to complete the questionnaire by offering a free programme for the following year's festival.

Festival directors and other staff are present at events throughout the festival period and this was stated as the principal means through which feedback was obtained. It was not the experience of organisers that audiences were reluctant to voice their opinions on festival events and on the programme generally. However, in the experience of a folk festival organiser, feedback is principally from the enthusiasts, whose views and expectations may differ from those of other festival goers. Some festivals give audiences the opportunity to provide feedback in 'meet the performer' sessions, in which festival organisers can participate and hear the views expressed.

The media provide an important source of feedback and, although some festivals find the media coverage they receive inadequate, some larger festivals receive in-depth coverage that can be helpful in planning later festivals. Even where coverage is limited, it can draw attention to a problem of which organisers may not have been fully aware. Other sources of feedback, on which evaluation is based, include other festival organisers and artists and, in the case of new or innovative works, the interest shown by organisers of other events in booking artists or groups on the basis of their festival performance. Success in this latter area is particularly gratifying to festival organisers, since it fulfils the objective of many festivals to encourage new work and innovation in the arts.

Priorities for development

It is evident from this study that many festival organisers regard the present period as one of change for festivals. Few festivals can afford to cater for a privileged minority of the population, and need to attract sections of the population that other arts promoters have failed to reach. Moreover, for many festivals, this consideration is not the result of financial expediency but a central objective in the festival's conception and development. Attracting a wide audience therefore informs many decisions made in festival organisation, including the artistic programme, marketing and ticketing policy. The influence of these factors was referred to in Chapter 3 and it is apparent that many festivals are particularly concerned at the age profile of their audience: their aim is to broaden the appeal of the festival to younger age groups. The need to attract younger people and to lay the foundations of a future festival audience is a central consideration behind festivals' involvement in educational work.

Attempts to attract greater numbers of working-class people appear to be less common and less well-formulated, as are attempts to attract ethnic minority groups. However, some festivals are making a concerted effort in both these respects: Llanelli and Bradford are supporting festival events in isolated working-class communities and, in the case of Bradford, actively encouraging participation by ethnic minority groups resident in the city.

Many festival organisers see the key to attracting uninitiated groups in the overall balance of the festival programme, and are therefore including or increasing the number of events in areas other than classical music. Folk festivals are also extending the range of musical forms traditionally covered to include roots, cajun and bluegrass. A central consideration behind this development has been the desire to attract a wider audience, and particularly to increase the proportion of young festival-goers.

The ability of festivals to succeed in achieving their aims for development will clearly depend on their financial resources. However, many festival organisers believe that they are in a position where they cannot develop further without additional funding and their inability to develop is threatening their survival. In Chapter 5 festivals' priorities for additional funding were examined. These include an extension of the festival period, extra staffing and better facilities for artists and the public. Festival organisers were also asked about their needs for improved venues.

Venues

Some festivals use a number of venues. Some are fortunate in having access to a wide range of venues suitable for staging the variety of performances and events featured in a typical arts festival. Others are restricted in scope and in the performances they can cover because suitable venues either do not exist or are unavailable. 30% of arts festivals take place largely or entirely at a single venue.

A festival's need for venues will clearly depend on the nature of performances featured, its audience and its general orientation. At the same time, the artistic programme of a festival is partly determined by the venues it has at its disposal. The Edinburgh International and Fringe festivals are fortunate in having access to a wide range of suitable venues, and this is a factor behind the successful development of these festivals. Two festivals included in the interview stage of our research, the Llanelli Festival and Camden Jazz, are restricted by limited access to venues with large seating capacity: the Llanelli Festival cannot invite large orchestras because the town's largest venue has fewer than 500 seats and such an event would incur a financial loss. Although suitable venues might be available to the Camden Jazz Festival in neighbouring boroughs, the organisers are reluctant to use them because the festival could thereby lose its identity and coherence.

Many organisers identified the principal unfulfilled need of festivals in this respect as a need for venues with a capacity of 700-900 for staging performances by known artists, including orchestral concerts, which have the potential to attract large audiences. However, this is by no means the only type of venue in short supply. Organisers report a need for even larger venues, but also for small venues with a capacity for audiences of around 100. These are much sought-after by groups appearing at the Edinburgh Festival Fringe.

Festival organisers have shown great ingenuity in identifying suitable buildings in their towns and cities, using churches, museums, hotels, private houses, rooms in pubs and, in the case of the Edinburgh Fringe, an operating theatre with viewing gallery, provided at the request of a drama group. The practice of using numerous venues can do much to promote the collective strength and celebratory atmosphere of a town during the festival period, raising its profile and reaching a potentially wider audience. However, organisers report a number of problems, including the availability of facilities and the relationship of the festival with the owners of venues. They frequently have to arrange for the temporary installation of sound and lighting equipment in some venues used for festivals. Again, refreshments can be difficult or virtually impossible to provide in some venues: for example, it may not be acceptable to set up a drinks bar inside a church. Facilities including bars and eating areas are particularly important where business sponsorship forms a substantial proportion of festival income and where sponsoring organisations want to use festival performance for hospitality purposes.

Poor catering facilities are by no means restricted to unconventional venues: many festival organisers reported that their principal, purpose-built, venue was in need of refurbishment to include these facilities and even to improve more basic features such as heating and decor.

Some festivals also expressed concern that the buildings they use do not offer easy access to wheel-chair users. This is particularly problematic where festivals use a range of venues that are not purpose built.

Finally, the availability of venues is as important as the presence of suitable buildings. Chapter 1 referred to the sale of local authority-owned venues and to the strong possibility that their management will be put out to tender. A number of festival organisers identified this as a threat to their festival. Several also complained about the attitude of some local venue owners who, they believe, see the festival as a chance to make money by charging excessive fees. There were also reports of conflict between venue owners and festival organisers where venues were permitted to stage festival events in their own right and charged ticket prices that the festival organisers considered excessive.

International developments

Numerous political and social developments have influenced, or are likely to affect, the direction that festivals take. Many festivals feature artists from outside the UK. Some have adopted the title of international festivals. Festival organisers were asked if international developments had any effect on the festival or were likely to do so in the future.

The festivals that include a substantial international element in their programmes find that it attracts considerable interest. It furthers the aim of many festivals to encourage new and innovative work in the arts. However, one festival organiser expressed the view that, in some cases, festivals have overstated their 'international' nature and have used an international theme or festival title principally for promotional purposes. Festival organisers saw considerable potential in increasing the diversity of international artistic forms for expanding the appeal of their festivals to younger people and to ethnic minority groups in particular. It is apparent that festivals see advantages for the local community in promoting international links: for example, the Llanelli Festival is currently involved in a twinning operation with a French town, which may lead to reciprocal invitations to artists and guests at the towns' festivals. There is also scope for the development of such links for sponsorship purposes: one festival organiser remarked on how a festival is an ideal time for a company to invite a foreign delegation.

During the 1980s there was considerable interest in the works of artists and groups from Eastern Europe. Festival organisers reported that their ability to include an Eastern European element was threatened by the removal of subsidies from these performers. More generally, musicians and other artists with an international reputation tend to view the UK as a less important stop on the international circuit than in the past. The circuit is now bigger and includes Japan where artists are achieving high sales of recorded music and can command high fees. Festival organisers referred to the relatively low level of subsidy to the arts in the UK in comparison with other European countries. In their experience, this has contributed to the difficulty of hiring international artists, particularly orchestras and celebrated performers.

A number of festival organisers remarked on the possible effects on arts festivals of the completion of the Single European Market in 1992. It was thought that the larger government subsidies provided by some other European countries might be a positive influence on arts funding in the UK. There was also a suggestion that the completion of the Single European Market might encourage sponsorship of UK arts festivals by non-British European companies. The Single European Market was also seen as an opportunity for British arts festivals to reach a wider audience and attract more publicity, particularly in areas where they are thought to be more advanced. The organiser of a puppet festival expressed the view that festival organisers in other European countries might be particularly interested in the success of a number of recently established British festivals in incorporating the cultural diversity of their host town or city.

Festivals' plans for change

In the postal survey festivals were asked if there were any plans for major changes in the nature of their festival. 29% answered yes to this question although, in some cases, the changes described could not be considered as of major proportions. General arts festivals were found to be most likely to be planning a change and classical music festivals least likely to be doing so. A number of festivals plan to change their organisational arrangements, including the date and duration of the festival and the venues used. Changes planned to the programme include a broadening to include a higher proportion of non-music events. Some festival organisers plan to introduce types of music not currently featured in the programme, including music which appeals to young people, such as roots and world music. This was reported by several folk festivals and by some arts festivals.

A number of festivals plan to increase attendances from people outside their area. They also aim to involve more members of the local community, and the two aims are not contradictory where festivals are aiming to increase audiences generally. Increased participation was raised by several festival organisers, who see the staging of more participatory or workshop events as the key to attracting a larger local audience. Related to this, some festival organisers also plan to hold more events for children.

The optimism of festival organisers

It is evident that festival organisers have ambitions for the future and are developing strategies accordingly. They were asked whether they were optimistic or pessimistic about the future of their festival and of arts festivals in general. The general feeling was one of optimism for their own festival, and a reluctance to comment on the general prospects for festivals.

Festivals receive feedback from audiences and from external sources, including the press, which, in some cases, is an important source of encouragement and for others the cause of frustration (see Chapter 4). The principal source of optimism among the festival organisers interviewed was seen as the enthusiasm of audiences, staff and participants. Festivals with a strong input from volunteers on the organisational or artistic side are particularly encouraged by this support because it provides them with a firm anchor: for example, the organisers of the Notting Hill Carnival are optimistic about its future because of the 'sheer energy, enthusiasm and optimism of the producers, costume makers and musicians'. Festivals that have achieved a popular following in their host town are generally optimistic that they will attract continuing support. But, in the long term, much depends on the success of their attempts to renew their audience, and some festivals feel that they must change in some way to achieve this.

Some festivals see a loyal audience as a sign of success: the organisers of two, very different, festivals, the Aldeburgh Festival and the Warwick Folk Festival, expressed the view that they have developed an audience that trusts the organisers to stage performances they will enjoy. This is achieved by skilful cultivation, as well as judgement, of audience tastes. Festival organisers do not generally regard themselves as merely responding to demand, but as in some way influencing it. The ability of festivals to attract artists of good standard and reputation is also considered a mark of success and a sign that the festival is taken seriously in the arts world and that it has a viable future.

The proliferation of arts festivals was an issue raised by many festival directors, one of whom expressed the view that, because it is portrayed by parts of the media as a 'bonanza of fun', the coverage given to the Edinburgh Festival had been partly responsible for this proliferation. Some directors found the proliferation encouraging, demonstrating the value and viability of the festival concept. One director saw festivals as part of the growing interest in the live arts, which was part of a conscious policy developed in the early 1980s to encourage a move away from passive and home-centred arts consumption (Bianchini, 1991). Others referred to the growing emphasis on participation in many festivals and, related to this, the growth in community festivals which are less focused on the classical arts than traditional arts festivals. These festivals have made more concentrated efforts to maximise access by staging as many out-of-door events as the British weather will permit and as many free events as their budgets allow.

Not all festival directors regard the proliferation of festivals as an entirely positive development. Some expressed the view that the number of festivals could reach 'saturation point', so that festivals would find increasing difficulty in competing for audiences, artists and funding. This could be particularly problematic for festivals of specialist interest which have a smaller pool of artists and audience to draw on, and for film festivals where a limited product is in demand from a growing number of festivals internationally.

The principal cause of pessimism among the festival organisers was the state of arts funding. Some organisers feel that they cannot expand, or keep their festival programme as interesting as they would like it to be, because they lack the financial resources to do so. Some report having to undertake an annual assessment of the festival's viability. For professionally run festivals, the uncertainty of funding is particularly bad for the morale of festival staff. Chapter 5 referred to some dissatisfaction with the funding of arts festivals through regional arts associations and boards. Some festival organisers are concerned at what they see as inadequate government support for arts festivals. More generally, a number expressed the view that their festival was undervalued in the local community, by potential funders and by the population generally. Some festivals are particularly critical of their local authority in this respect, and some believe that inadequate support from the media is one important factor in this (see Chapter 4).

Among festivals that are local authority run, the principal cause of pessimism was stated to be the uncertainty surrounding continuation of funding, without which the festival could probably not survive. Organisers of these festivals are not aware of a lack of support for the festival in principle, but recognise that the arts are not a priority for expenditure and that local authorities are experiencing increasing difficulty in delivering even their statutory services. The uncertainty surrounding local authority funding has therefore led some festival organisers to question their authority's ultimate commitment to the festival.

The success of a number of high profile festivals has encouraged recognition of the importance of festivals to the nation's cultural life, and this has benefitted smaller festivals. This awareness has not been restricted to their artistic importance but has included their economic value. It has been an important consideration behind the support given to arts festivals by local authorities which have recognised the importance of a town's image not only to tourists and to enhancing the quality of life for local residents, but also to local economic development. The arts have been consciously used in some cities as one means of improving a city's image. Glasgow, Birmingham and Bradford have all staged major arts events, including festivals, for this purpose.

Conclusions

The proliferation of arts festivals and the relatively young age of the majority of festivals suggest that they are considered to be an appropriate use of arts funding. The origins and impetus behind the growth of arts festivals varies from festival to festival and many of their benefits, including improvement in the quality of life and in promoting economic development, are difficult to measure with any degree of accuracy. Some of the more tangible benefits are their role in attracting income for the arts, the generation of employment, and the encouragement of amateur involvement and of voluntary activity in the arts.

Three issues raised in this report deserve particular attention and consideration. They are the role of festivals in commissioning new work, their educational role, and business sponsorship of arts festivals.

Many festival organisers see festivals as having an important role to play in commissioning new work. A festival can give exposure to new artists, and the public may be more inclined to attend such performances during a festival. A third of all festivals commission new work but it is a costly activity and the festivals that do so have higher levels of public subsidy. Many festival organisers feel that they could make a greater contribution in this area if they had a higher level of guaranteed funding.

Many festival organisers regard their festival as having a role to play in education, even if only in the broadest sense of widening access to arts performances and events. People may be attracted to arts venues or to performances which they would not usually attend at other times of the year. In addition, many festivals have provided an explicitly educational content. As with the commissioning of new work, festivals with higher levels of income from public sources have a greater involvement in educational work than other festivals. Behind this involvement is an awareness of the need to build a new festival audience and to lower the current age profile of many festival audiences. Many festivals therefore include children's events in addition to an educational component, and aim also to attract parents who do not currently attend arts festivals. The level of involvement of festivals in educational work suggests that festivals have a proven success in this area, but there is also a need for funding and guidance in this involvement.

Festivals attract an estimated £6.8 million in business sponsorship each year and are increasingly reliant on funding from this source. Business sponsorship is no substitute for public funding, since by its nature it cannot be guaranteed. However, for many festivals it represents a substantial proportion of total income and, despite the recession, festival organisers believe that there is scope for increased levels of business sponsorship. Many festival organisers lack the skills or resources to promote business sponsorship and are in need of assistance in this area of income generation.

The present period is one of change for festivals and the next ten years will probably see the emergence of new festivals and the demise of some existing ones. Festivals will certainly continue to make a substantial contribution to the enjoyment of, and participation in, the arts and to occupy a unique position in the cultural life of the nation.

Key points

- Festival organisers use a range of methods for evaluating the success of their festival, including audience surveys, attendances, organised discussions during the festival and media coverage.

- Some festivals are making a concerted effort to attract social groups which are currently under-represented in festival audiences, including young people, working class people and people from ethnic minority groups.

- Many festivals are fortunate in having access to a wide range of suitable venues and the variety of festival performances and events allows for a range of venues to be used. However, festivals have unfulfilled needs for venues of particular types and the principal need is for venues with a capacity of 700-900.

- Some festival organisers believe that the relatively low level of public subsidy to the arts in the UK, in comparison with other European countries, has contributed towards the difficulty they experience in hiring international artists. Some are optimistic that the completion of a Single European Market may exert a favourable influence.

- 29% of festival organisers are planning to make changes in the nature of their festival, and general arts festivals are more likely than others to be doing so. Changes were planned in the date, duration and venues used and changes planned to the programme included a broadening out to include a higher proportion of non-musical events and music with a particular appeal to young people.

- The principal cause of optimism among festival organisers is the enthusiasm of audiences, staff and participants.

- The principal cause of pessimism among festival organisers is the state of arts funding.

- Some festival organisers believe that tough competition for funding discourages festivals from including innovatory work and makes festivals' programmes increasingly predictable and unadventurous.

References

Aldeburgh Foundation (1987) *The Aldeburgh Story.*

Bianchini, Franco (1991) 'Urban Cultural Policy', Discussion Document, National Arts and Media Strategy, Arts Council.

Curtis, Ruth and Henderson, Gavin (1991) 'Festivals', Discussion Document, National Arts and Media Strategy, Arts Council.

Hutchison, Robert and Forester, Susan (1987) *Arts Centres in the United Kingdom*, Policy Studies Institute, 1987.

Hutchison, Robert and Feist, Andrew (1991) *Amateur Arts in the UK: the PSI survey of amateur arts and crafts in the UK*, Policy Studies Institute.

Millward Brown International (1991) *Pricing the Arts Report 1990* commissioned by the Arts Council and Scottish Arts Council, February.

Myerscough, John et al. (1988) *The Economic Importance of the Arts in Britain*, Policy Studies Institute.

Office of Arts and Libraries (1990) *Volunteers in Museums and Heritage Organisations: Policy, planning and management*, HMSO.

Scottish Tourist Board (1992) *Edinburgh Festivals Study: Visitor survey and economic impact assessment.*

Appendix 1

Arts Festivals in the UK

A national study by the independent

Policy Studies Institute

POLICY STUDIES INSTITUTE

100 PARK VILLAGE EAST, LONDON NWI 3SR
TEL: 071-387 2171   FAX: 071-388 0914

Arts Festivals in the UK

Important

Please read before answering the questions

Please answer the questions by ticking the appropriate box(es) or writing in your answer as indicated. Some of the questions ask for numbers and percentages. **If exact figures are not available please provide estimates based on your personal judgement.**

The main part of the questionnaire asks about your festival's activities, staffing, audience and attendances. Questions on finance are covered on a separate sheet. **All questions refer to the most recent festival unless otherwise stated.**

All answers will be treated in confidence. No individual festival will be identified in the report of the survey without the organisers' prior permission.

When you have completed the questionnaire please return it in the pre-paid envelope provided. Ideally we would like you to return both parts of the questionnaire together, but if there is an unavoidable delay in obtaining information for the finance questionnaire, please send it on later.

If you experience any difficulty completing the questionnaire or would like further information, please contact Dr Heather Rolfe at the Policy Studies Institute (071-387 2171).

Arts Festivals in the United Kingdom

A survey by the independent Policy Studies Institute

All questions refer to the most recent festival unless otherwise stated.

What is the name of the festival? ....

Please would you provide your name, address and telephone number

....
....
....
....

SECTION 1 – ACTIVITIES

1. What would be the most appropriate description of the festival (e.g. arts festival, jazz festival, carnival)?

    ....

2. When was the festival first held?

    Year [   ]

3. When was your most recent festival?

    Month [   ]   Year [   ]

4. What was the duration of the festival? (*please tick appropriate box*)

    2-3 days [   ]
    4-7days [   ]
    8-14 days [   ]

    Other (*please specify*)

    ....

5. How often is the festival held? *(please tick appropriate box)*

Annually ☐

Biennially ☐

Other *(please specify)*

. . . .

6. Was the festival based in one venue (e.g. an arts centre)?

Yes ☐

No ☐

7a. Were festival events linked by a common theme?

Yes ☐ Q7b

No ☐ Q8

7b. If yes, what was the theme?

. . . .

8a. Did the festival include activities for adults other than arts events, performances and exhibitions? (e.g. guided walks, lectures)

Yes ☐ Q8b

No ☐ Q9

8b. If yes, what proportion of the festival was devoted to the arts?

☐ %

9. In answering this question please exclude any special programme for children and performances in a fringe festival.

a) Which art forms did the most recent festival cover?
(please tick appropriate boxes in column a)

b) How many arts **performances/events/exhibitions** were held in each category?
(please provide approximate figures in column b)

	a) Included in festival	b) Total no of performances/events exhibitions held in this category
Music		
Orchestral	☐	☐
Choral	☐	☐
Chamber/soloist	☐	☐

Jazz ☐ ☐

Folk ☐ ☐

Rock/Pop ☐ ☐

Other music (*please specify*) ☐ ☐

. . . .

. . . .

Opera ☐ ☐

Musicals/light opera ☐ ☐

Dance

Classical ballet ☐ ☐

Contemporary ☐ ☐

Folk/ethnic ☐ ☐

Other dance (*please specify*) ☐ ☐

. . . .

. . . .

Carnival ☐ ☐

Mime ☐ ☐

Drama ☐ ☐

Cabaret/Comedy ☐ ☐

Puppetry ☐ ☐

Film ☐ ☐

Literature/poetry ☐ ☐

Craft ☐ ☐

Visual arts ☐ ☐

Other (*please specify other arts events not listed above*)

. . . .

. . . .

10a. Please give your estimate of the **numbers** of artists, professional and amateur who performed at the most recent festival:

Professional ☐

Amateur ☐

10b. Please estimate the proportion of events which involved professionals, amateurs or both:

Proportion of events involving
professional artists only [   ] %

Proportion of events involving
amateur artists only [   ] %

Proportion of events involving
professional and amateur artists [   ] %

11. Were the artists who performed at the festival:

Chiefly from the local community? [   ]

Chiefly from other areas of the UK or abroad? [   ]

A mixture of both? [   ]

12. Was there a fringe festival at the same time as the main festival?

Yes [   ]

No [   ]

13a. Did the most recent festival include a special programme/events for children?

Yes [   ] Q13b

No [   ] Q14

13b. If yes, how many performances/events/exhibitions did the children's
programme contain?

[   ]

14. Did the festival commission any new work?

Yes [   ]

No [   ]

15a. Did the festival have any explicit educational component?

Yes [   ] Q15b

No [   ] Q16

15b. If yes, what form did this take?

. . . .

SECTION 2 – ORGANISATION AND STAFFING

16. What type of constitution did the festival have?
    (please tick relevant box/boxes)

    Local authority ☐
    Festival trust ☐
    Ad-hoc festival committee ☐
    Company limited by guarantee ☐
    Other *(please specify)* ☐

    ....
    ....

17. Who decided the main artistic programme of the festival (e.g. festival director, festival committee)?

    ....

18. How many people were involved in the **organisation** of the festival as paid employees?
    (please provide approximate figures)

    (a) Full-time ☐
    (b) Part-time ☐

19. How many people were involved in the organisation of the festival as volunteers?

    (a) Volunteers for the period of the festival only ☐

    (b) Volunteers during the festival and throughout the year ☐

20. Were volunteers from a festival friends association?

    Yes ☐
    No ☐

21. What proportion of paid festival employees were permanent or temporary?
    (please approximate proportions)

    (a) Permanent (employed for 12 months of the year) ☐ %
    (b) Temporary (employed for the festival season only) ☐ %

22. What proportion of paid festival employees were self-employed? [   ] %

23. Were any festival staff seconded from business?

Yes [   ]
No [   ]

24. Did the festival provide placements to people on government training schemes?

Yes [   ]
No [   ]

25. Did the festival use outside contractors?

Yes [   ]
No [   ]

26. What duties did paid employees, volunteers and staff employed by outside contractors carry out? (*please tick relevant boxes*)

	Paid employees	Volunteers	Contract staff
Administration/organisation	[ ]	[ ]	[ ]
Publicity	[ ]	[ ]	[ ]
Sales/box office	[ ]	[ ]	[ ]
Secretarial	[ ]	[ ]	[ ]
Catering	[ ]	[ ]	[ ]
Cleaning	[ ]	[ ]	[ ]
Stewarding at events	[ ]	[ ]	[ ]
Fund raising	[ ]	[ ]	[ ]
Other (*please specify*)	[ ]	[ ]	[ ]

....
....
....
....

SECTION 3 – AUDIENCES AND ATTENDANCES

27. Have any surveys of audiences and attendances been carried out at the festival in the period 1986-1991?

Yes ☐
No ☐

Please enclose copies of any available reports when you return this questionnaire.

28. What was the estimated total audience for the most recent festival including free events? *(please provide approximate figures)*

(a) Number of tickets sold for all events at the festival ☐

(b) Number of attendances at free events ☐

29. How did these figures compare with 5 years ago (1986)? *(please tick appropriate boxes)*

	Higher than in 1986	Lower than in 1986	About the same	Not known
Number of people attending festival	☐	☐	☐	☐
Number of tickets sold for all events at the festival	☐	☐	☐	☐

30. Was the festival audience:

largely local? ☐
largely from outside the area? ☐
Not known ☐

31. Was the festival content designed to attract tourists to the festival?

Yes ☐
No ☐

32a. Was the festival content designed with particular sections of the population in mind?

Yes ☐ Q32b
No ☐ Q33a

32b. If yes, what sections of the population did the festival programme aim to attract?

....

....

33a. Were any festival performances or events broadcast on radio or television?
(*please tick appropriate box*)

Yes ☐ Q33b
No ☐ Q34a

33b. If yes, how many performances or events were broadcast?

Radio broadcasts ☐
Television broadcasts ☐

34a. Are there any plans for major changes in the nature of the festival?

Yes ☐ Q34b
No ☐ Q35

34b. If yes, what are these changes?

....

....

35. If there is anything you would like to add to your answers, or anything you would like to say about arts festivals, we would welcome your comments.

Please would you return your completed questionnaire in the pre-paid envelope provided.

Thank you very much for your help

Arts Festivals in the United Kingdom

A survey by the independent Policy Studies Institute

Part 2 of questionnaire

FINANCES

1. What is the name of the festival? ....

2. Please give the main items of income and expenditure for the most recent festival:

Operating Income	£	**Operating Expenditure**	£
Box office		Professional artists' fees	
Business sponsorship		Festival staff salaries	
Local authority/ local arts council		Other administration expenses	
Regional arts association		Publicity/marketing	
National arts council		Venue and equipment hire	
Friends' Association		Royalties	
Donations		Other expenditure (eg hospitality)	
Other earned income (eg from catering, sales of goods or programmes)			
Total income		Total expenditure	

3. Did you incur a deficit on your most recent festival?

   Yes ☐
   No ☐

4. Does the festival have an accumulated deficit?

   Yes ☐
   No ☐

5. Does the festival receive any support **in kind** from a local authority?

Yes ☐

No ☐

6. Does the festival receive any support **in kind** from business?

Yes ☐

No ☐

7. If your answer to either question 5 or question 6 is yes, what does this support consist of? (*please tick appropriate boxes*)

	Local authority	Business
Seconding of staff to the festival	☐	☐
Use of premises for performances	☐	☐
Use of premises for organisation/ administration	☐	
Publicity	☐	☐
Equipment	☐	☐

Other (*please specify*)

. . . .

. . . .

. . . .

. . . .

8a. Have there been any major changes in your sources of income over the last five years? (since 1986)

Yes ☐ Q8b

No ☐ end

8b. If yes, please say what these have been:

. . . .

. . . .

. . . .

Thank you very much for your help

Arts Festivals in the United Kingdom

A survey by the independent Policy Studies Institute

All questions refer to the most recent festival unless otherwise stated.

What is the name of the festival?   . . . .

Please would you provide your name, address and telephone number

. . . .
. . . .
. . . .
. . . .

1. When was the festival first held?

Year [ ]

2. When was your most recent festival?

Month [ ]   Year [ ]

3. What was the duration of the festival? (*please tick appropriate box*)

2-3 days [ ]
4-7days [ ]
8-14 days [ ]
Other (*please specify*)
. . . .

4. How often is the festival held? (*please tick appropriate box*)

Annually [ ]
Biennially [ ]
Other (*please specify*)
. . . .

5. Was the festival based in one venue (e.g. an arts centre)?

Yes [ ]
No [ ]

6a. Were festival events linked by a common theme?

Yes ☐ Q6b

No ☐ Q7

6b. If yes, what was the theme?

. . . .

7. Would you please estimate the total number of performances and events at the most recent festival: ☐

8a. Please give your estimate of the **numbers** of artists, professional and amateur who performed at the most recent festival:

Professional ☐

Amateur ☐

8b. Please estimate the proportion of events which involved professionals, amateurs or both:

Proportion of events involving professional artists only ☐ %

Proportion of events involving amateur artists only ☐ %

Proportion of events involving professional and amateur artists ☐ %

9. Were the artists who performed at the festival:

Chiefly from the local community? ☐

Chiefly from other areas of the UK or abroad? ☐

A mixture of both? ☐

10a. Did the most recent festival include a special programme/events for children?

Yes ☐ Q10b

No ☐ Q11

10b. If yes, how many performances/events/exhibitions did the children's programme contain? ☐

11. What type of constitution did the festival have?
    (*please tick relevant box/boxes*)

    Local authority ☐
    Festival trust ☐
    Ad-hoc festival committee ☐
    Company limited by guarantee ☐
    Other (*please specify*) ☐

    ....
    ....

12. Who decided the main artistic programme of the festival (e.g. festival director, festival committee)?

    ....

13. How many people were involved in the **organisation** of the festival as paid employees?
    (*please provide approximate figures*)

    (a) Full-time ☐
    (b) Part-time ☐

14. How many people were involved in the organisation of the festival as volunteers?

    (a) Volunteers for the period
    of the festival only ☐

    (b) Volunteers during the festival
    and throughout the year ☐

15. Were volunteers from a festival friends association?

    Yes ☐
    No ☐

16. What was the estimated total audience for the most recent festival including free events?
    (*please provide approximate figures*)

    (a) Number of tickets sold
    for all events at the festival ☐
    (b) Number of attendances at free events ☐

17. How did these figures compare with 5 years ago (1986)? *(please tick appropriate boxes)*

	Higher than in 1986	Lower than in 1986	About the same	Not known
Number of people attending festival	☐	☐	☐	☐
Number of tickets sold for all events at the festival	☐	☐	☐	☐

18. Was the festival audience:

largely local? ☐

largely from outside the area? ☐

Not known ☐

19. Was the festival content designed to attract tourists to the festival?

Yes ☐

No ☐

20a. Was the festival content designed with particular sections of the population in mind?

Yes ☐ Q20b

No ☐ Q21a

20b. If yes, what sections of the population did the festival programme aim to attract?

. . . .

. . . .

21a. Are there any plans for major changes in the nature of the festival?

Yes ☐ Q21b

No ☐ Q22

21b. If yes, what are these changes?

. . . .

. . . .

22. If there is anything you would like to add to your answers, or anything you would like to say about arts festivals, we would welcome your comments.

Please would you return your completed questionnaire in the pre-paid envelope provided.

Thank you very much for your help

Appendix 2

Estimation of totals

The response rate to the survey was 66%. In addition, some respondents were unable to provide financial information. To produce an estimate of total income and total ticket sales for all arts festivals in the UK required survey data to be grossed up or weighted.

The range of festival income and size is wide, and the large festivals, although few in number, account for a substantial proportion of total income and total ticket sales. To produce a realistic estimated total, respondents were grouped into size bands. Each size band was then weighted inversely to its estimated response rate. We knew that response from the largest festivals was almost complete, and it was reasonable to assume progressively declining response rates from smaller festivals. Uniform weighting would have inflated the contribution of the larger festivals and led to an overall over-estimate. The method adopted here is likely, if anything, to lead to a conservative estimate.

Estimated totals of income from business sponsorship, regional arts boards, and local authorities and local arts associations were calculated by applying the average (mean) proportion of income reported under these headings to the total income as estimated above.